Redefining Innovation
Embracing the 80-80 Rule
to Ignite Growth in the
Biopharmaceutical Industry

Redefining Innovation

Embracing the 80-80 Rule to Ignite Growth in the Biopharmaceutical Industry

Ruchin Kansal
Jeff Huth

A PRODUCTIVITY PRESS BOOK

Routledge
Taylor & Francis Group
711 Third Avenue, New York, NY 10017

© 2018 by Ruchin Kansal and Jeff Huth
Productivity Press is an imprint of Taylor & Francis Group, an Informa business

No claim to original U.S. Government works

Printed on acid-free paper

International Standard Book Number-13: 978-1-138-58104-3 (Hardback)

Visit the Taylor & Francis Web site at
http://www.taylorandfrancis.com

and the Productivity Press site at
http://www.ProductivityPress.com

Contents

Reviews

"The biopharmaceutical industry, in general, has lagged behind in embracing the potential of rapidly evolving healthcare technology. To remain relevant, it needs to redefine its role and value proposition in the broader healthcare ecosystem. *Redefining Innovation* challenges conventional wisdom in which the traditional focus has been on the creation and launch of blockbuster drugs. The new focus can and should be around how digital health solutions may be applied in conjunction with medications to optimize care delivery and improve health outcomes."

David Rhew, M.D., Chief Medical Officer and Head of Healthcare and Fitness, Samsung Electronics America

"The authors make a strong case in describing the difficulties faced by many biopharmaceutical companies in redefining their Innovation Agenda, which today is almost exclusively focused on developing and commercializing products. Their perspective on broadening the way incumbents approach innovation will be a great gap-filler."

Marcus Wilson, President, HealthCore

"The 80-80 Rule creates urgency for Senior Leadership to redefine, communicate, and champion their organization's Innovation Agenda."

William Fleming, President, Healthcare Services, Humana

"Given the nature and magnitude of the challenges ahead of us in truly improving healthcare in the United States, we need less fragmentation and more collaboration and partnering. Messrs. Kansal and Huth have described this opportunity based on their personal experience in setting up cross-functional collaborations across the ecosystem."

Dr. David Feinberg, President and Chief Executive Officer, Geisinger

"Overall I find this book to be a refreshing perspective from biopharma insiders that are trying to help their industry sector renew its business. It will be a great platform for meaningful dialog around the future of healthcare and the role that the biopharma industry will play."

Ed Yu, Chairman, Vascular Cures and Retired Partner, Strategy & (PwC)

"*Redefining Innovation* puts forth a compelling argument about why the standard operating procedures of the past will not provide a sustainable pathway to future success. The 80-80 Rule serves as a blueprint which can be applied beyond the biopharma industry and should be taken seriously by all sectors within healthcare as well as other industries clinging to past glory."

Dr. Z. Colette Edwards, Managing Editor of the ***Wharton Healthcare Quarterly*, the journal of the Wharton Health Care Management Alumni Association**

"Over the past few years, I have seen a gradual increase in the willingness of biopharma leaders to engage in exploring new types of relationships with health systems. We are discussing collaborative projects to ensure adequate representation of diverse populations in clinical trials, outcomes-based reimbursement models, and health improvement opportunities beyond the pharmaceutical product. Success with these initiatives support the authors' recommendations for biopharmaceutical manufacturers to examine and transform both their historical approach to innovation and current business model."

Michael J Dowling, President and CEO Northwell Health

"The authors challenge the mainstream biopharmaceutical industry to consider whether recent gaps relative to its historical track record of success may require a broader definition of innovation. At the same time, I am very encouraged by the opportunity for companies engaged in breakthrough science and technology coupled with innovation in the areas of pricing, reimbursement and market access models to treat and potentially cure serious and life-threatening conditions, where limited therapeutic options have existed to date."

Joseph La Barge, Chief Legal Officer - Spark Therapeutics

Setting the Context

The Merriam Webster dictionary defines innovation as the introduction of something new, or a new idea, method, or device. In the business context, innovation is the introduction of something new to increase or create new sources of revenue.

We have focused our discussion on the biopharmaceutical industry, with an emphasis on subsectors that develop drugs that are either chemically derived or biologics. (Other subsectors include generics, biosimilars, over the counter medications (OTC), precision medicine, and regenerative medicine.)[1] In this context, we define innovation for the biopharmaceutical industry up to the present time as that focused exclusively on the discovery and development of biopharmaceutical products (typically referred to as R&D) for administration to patients in the home or clinical settings. In the past, such innovation contributed to the creation of what we call a Unicorn Industry, but it's profit model is now challenged, and it needs to examine new sources of innovation that go beyond the traditional biopharmaceutical product. We propose a new, future industry subsector, Smart integrated Medicine or S[i]M, with the potential to disrupt not only the historical product value proposition, but also the business model of the industry.

Endnote

1. The Pharmaceutical and Biotech Industries in the United States. Accessed January 19, 2018. https://www.selectusa.gov/pharmaceutical-and-biotech-industries-united-states

Foreword

Just over a year ago, I sat at a table in midtown Manhattan, waiting for my lunch guest to arrive. It was raining heavily outside, and the restaurant was busy with type-A professionals squeezing in a quick meal and power meeting, so I chose a table off to the side where we'd be able to better talk. Ruchin had asked me to meet to discuss some ideas he had on the topic of innovation, and a problem he and his colleague Jeff wanted to tackle. At the time, Ruchin and Jeff were deeply involved with innovation initiatives at Boehringer Ingelheim, an organization I had worked with for many years in my capacity as CEO of an innovation research and training firm. Ruchin and I had known each other for several years and had bonded over the topic of innovation—particularly, on why it seemed so hard for companies to sustain innovation over time. Why was it that so many players in the biopharma industry, once known for their revolutionary approach to medicine, were now lagging behind? With so many talented people and resources at their disposal, why were these organizations unable to sustain innovation as a driving force for their success? This is what we spent our time discussing. An hour soon passed and we were barely scratching the surface with our thoughts and stories.

Ironically, I told Ruchin, I had just arrived home on a redeye that morning from Europe, where my company led a multi-day training session on Leading Innovation at a large biopharmaceutical company. There were over 100 people in attendance, each more accomplished than the next, from a wide range of backgrounds: a procurement team, a legal team, a brand group. The company had identified "Innovation" as one of their strategic pillars and was actively rolling out training across the company to help teams "be more innovative" so that innovation was no longer seen as solely the job of R&D; it was everybody's job to create new growth for the company. To do this, innovation had to be thought of more broadly than just "products," and people had to get comfortable with taking smart risks. My team's job was to help them accomplish this. The work was hugely rewarding, but frankly extremely challenging. Why? Because a paradigm exists within many biopharma companies today: quite often the very same leaders that hire us to come in and teach innovation to their teams are the very people that hold us back from doing it when we arrive. They want us to teach teams to be more innovative, but not take too big of a risk; they want people to embrace new ideas, as long as they don't distract too much from the core business; they want to build a culture of innovation, but largely believe that the occasional Shark Tank contest or colorful walls in meeting rooms would be enough to accomplish this. I think anyone reading this is probably smiling and nodding at this point, having had similar experiences at their own organizations and knowing full well that's not how innovation works.

Twenty years ago, I started my innovation firm, future**think**, to help people eradicate the complexities that hold organizations back from valuable work and teach them the skills to unlock broader ideas for growth in their businesses. Most often, leaders come to us for help because something's stalled: the organization was once innovative— disruptive even—but as it grew and became more successful this became harder to do. The original innovative drive that put these people on the map and defined who they were was now difficult to achieve consistently, if at all. Was it due to scale? The drive to meet short-term earnings? The pace of change and the impact of keeping up with constantly evolving technologies? Growing regulations? Or human risk aversion? The answer of course, as Ruchin and I discussed, was yes.

At many companies in their early stages, and not just in biopharma, the most innovative organizations and their leaders seem unstoppable. They are geniuses with incredible ideas, high risk tolerances, and products and services that are transforming the industry and dramatically improving outcomes. But typically, in less than a decade, an irony soon emerges. The now incumbents, once thought of as disruptive innovators, start to operate using mostly status quo approaches—the "knowns"—versus the unknowns. They begin to lean heavily toward evolution and minimize revolution. Complacency sets in, and this becomes their potential downfall. One only needs to think about RIM with its Blackberry, Yahoo!, Nokia, Sears, or Blockbuster to know what I'm talking about.

What needs to change? This book examines this issue in brilliant detail. The biopharma industry focuses an overwhelming amount of its efforts on drug development, at a time when the healthcare industry has become far broader than that. It has moved beyond this almost singular focus to embrace technologies, customer experiences, services, and business models that make up a more complete ecosystem of care. As the authors point out, this presents a tremendous opportunity to those that wish to expand their view; and presents a potential death knell to those that don't. Imagine if Apple was still focused only on computers? Or if car companies like BMW were only focused on manufacturing cars versus offering new ride share services or mobility systems? Organizations like these are successful because they have instilled a mindset that proactively recognizes and reacts to changes in the broader economy and society. They continually explore spaces adjacent to and beyond their current methods of doing business. For example, we know that car companies actively hire software engineers, not just mechanical ones; they explore unexpected partnerships with technology companies and even with urban planners to transform cities and their transportation systems. Should the biopharma industry not think and act the same way to achieve new growth?

This book is a call to arms for those engaged in the innovation agenda in an organization. It provides a path forward to transform the processes, decision-making, and overall culture to better embrace innovation not as a part of the organization, but as a cornerstone of it. While creating blockbuster drugs is without question important to improving lives and patient outcomes, it can no longer be the overwhelming majority of what the industry provides. If it does, leaders will be caught off guard by the nimbler, forward-looking outsiders that see new opportunities—and aggressively act on them.

Authors Ruchin Kansal and Jeff Huth challenge the current operating approaches within the biopharma industry by questioning what we view as "innovative." They show how we as leaders and innovators can take better risks, and then offer a blueprint for culture change so that practitioners at all levels will expand their view and try new things—and so that the resulting innovation portfolio, while it will include some misses, will also result in a wider variety of successes.

Leveraging their unique experiences tackling similar challenges and opportunities at one of the top 15 global biopharma companies, and complemented by conversations with leaders across the healthcare ecosystem, the pages that follow clearly articulate the underlying reasons the industry has been slow in responding to driving forces in the healthcare system. They highlight the tensions between the desire to maintain the status quo versus the need to embrace the new by taking readers through a journey into the history of the biopharma industry which they characterize as a "Unicorn Industry" given that most products launched by biopharma companies achieve greater than a billion dollars in revenue. They cleverly explore how frameworks that classify innovation as core, adjacent, and breakthrough can guide incumbents' self-examination toward defining their optimal approach to innovation—and stretch their thinking in productive ways. Importantly, Ruchin and Jeff introduce the idea of Smart integrated Medicine or S[i]M and the RKJH2018 Standards that can guide the evolution and adoption of S[i]M in the market and create the foundation for the next generation of innovators that embraces new technology, supported by novel reimbursement and commercial models to participate more broadly in the healthcare system.

Finally, they introduce a compelling approach that leaders can embrace to drive experimentation, smarter risk taking, and better innovation results: The 80-80 Rule. It states that "being 80% confident that you will only be 80% right the first time should feel normal" as the basis for transforming the culture and risk propensity at biopharma incumbents to pave new futures. I believe 80-80 is not just a rule but rather a mindset that can be embraced not just within the biopharma industry, but for those struggling with innovation in other industries as well.

For those looking to move the needle in their own organization, your journey to success began when you started this book. Its contents will surely ignite your inherent drive for creating positive change and new value that is so needed to ensure a better future. I hope you enjoy this read as much as I did.

Lisa Bodell
Founder and CEO, future**think**
Bestselling Author, *Why Simple Wins, Kill the Company*

Preface

Growing up in India

I (Ruchin) grew up in India. I distinctly remember the day we received the news that my grandfather had died. I was in the 6th grade. One of the first civil engineers of Indian origin to have graduated in post-British India—from Thomason College of Civil Engineering in the scenic town of Roorkee at the foot of the Himalayas. He had retired at the top of the food chain in the Public Works Department for the state of Uttar Pradesh. I remember riding on his back when I was little and on the red leather seats of the brand-new Ambassador car that he bought upon retirement—a luxury in the 1980s in India. I remember him, all dressed up in white, making little scorebooks for the cricket matches we used to have in our backyard. One morning while out for a walk, he collapsed and died. The cause of death: heart attack. It was a shock: he was healthy, physically fit, an avid tennis player, a teetotaler, and had a balanced vegetarian diet. He rarely went to see the doctor. After his death, physical check-ups became the norm in our family. We realized that high blood-pressure and coronary artery disease ran in the family and were the most likely reason for his heart attack. My mother was diagnosed with high blood-pressure when she was in her mid-fifties, but anti-hypertensives, another innovation of the biopharmaceutical industry, allow her to keep her blood-pressure under control. She is now 71 and can outrun me any day.

My brother and I had a case of typhoid once and that we had to live on bitter gourd juice for 15 days. We survived because there were antibiotics available to treat the disease. Still, more than 21 million people die of typhoid each year just because they don't have access to antibiotics. My son suffers from asthma, which is potentially life-threatening even today for people with no access to medication. We sleep well because we know his medication works, his breathing tests have improved, and he can fully participate in biking—his favorite outdoor activity—all year. My neighbor was recently on a 15-hour flight from New York to Dubai. Her daughter had a little rash before they boarded the plane, but they ignored it as a simple bug bite. Once in the air, she had a severe anaphylactic reaction in the form of a rash that was spreading very fast. The airline crew was able to transmit a picture of the rash to the ground medical staff, who immediately prescribed diphenhydramine—a drug so common that even the airline crew typically carries it as part of its first aid kit. Upon administration, the rash was gone within minutes, and the family was able to continue their journey without any further incident.

Growing up in the United States

Through the eyes of a child growing up in the United States in the 50s and 60s, my (Jeff) initial experience with healthcare was shaped by a sole practice General Practitioner (GP) who routinely made house calls 10 miles from his office. I never heard about medical expenses in the household as they were covered by my father's employer-sponsored health insurance. I had 3 of 4 grandparents live into their 90s thanks to a relatively healthy lifestyle, and, just as importantly, readily available and relatively affordable healthcare. Fast forward 50 years and I now find myself helping older relatives navigate an increasingly fragmented and complex system in which several different providers employed by large, corporatized healthcare organizations can't or won't communicate with each other. Healthcare bills require a CPA to understand, and costs in the form of premiums, deductibles, co-pays, and out-of-pocket balances increase well beyond the rate of income growth. Nearly everyone in that age group now looks back with nostalgia and longs for the days of the roving GP and the neighborhood pharmacist.

In parallel, I have seen the industry in which I worked for almost 40 years, during what could be considered the heyday of pharmaceutical development and commercialization, go through massive changes. Once highly regarded by the public and the "favorite son" of Wall Street we now find the biopharmaceutical industry facing significant pressure from many environmental factors, disruption from outside and, perhaps in the most extreme case, obsolescence. While I am incredibly proud of the work our industry continues to do every day, in social settings I find myself no longer able to trumpet the novel treatments and even cures delivered by our industry. Instead, I have to increasingly defend Direct-to-Consumer (DTC) advertising, questionable marketing practices, and the rising cost of branded biopharmaceuticals.

The biopharmaceutical industry is rooted in innovation. Innovation in the industry typically refers to research, discovery, and development (RD&D or simply R&D) of synthetic molecules or biological prescription drug products (pills, injections, and infusions), traditionally referred to as ethical biopharmaceuticals. It's the industry that eradicated, eliminated, or reduced diseases like plague, smallpox, chicken pox, cholera, polio—conditions that have in the past wiped out entire civilizations. It's the industry that gave the world insulin, penicillin, the birth control pill, ACE inhibitors, statins, paracetamol, and ibuprofen. We live better because biopharmaceutical products help us manage common chronic conditions and diseases like infections, diabetes, and hypertension that were fatal not so long ago. They have become such an integral part of everyday lives that we don't realize how effective they are until they are not easily accessible. Imagine a simple case of allergy without antihistamine, an asthmatic without his inhaler, a diabetic without her insulin, someone suffering from blood clotting disorders without blood thinners, someone suffering from anxiety disorders without anxiolytics. More recently the industry has been responsible for bringing forth innovative medicines for cancer, immunological diseases, and rare diseases that are giving individuals and families reasons to cheer, live, and celebrate life. These are the marvels of modern biopharmaceuticals. At the same time, there are many more diseases that still need effective treatments—from fighting new, resistant infections to eradicating cancer and solving for mental health challenges—and the industry holds the competency to address these diseases. The critical question is whether the competencies and business model that enabled the historical progress we all marvel at will be sufficient going forward.

The story of the biopharmaceutical industry is also one in which a confluence of multiple disconnected events led to the formation of what we term a "Unicorn Industry" in the United States. A peak in biopharmaceutical innovation, maturing of the employer-based payment model, and regulation governing prescribing authority and patent protection all came together at the same time in the early 1990s. The unanticipated result was the unicorn business model of the industry that would lead to the creation of multiple blockbusters—products with annual revenues exceeding $1 billion year after year for an entire sector. The business model became the growth engine of the industry.

This traditional R&D-based growth engine is starting to stutter. Anywhere you turn, the industry is under siege today. There are discussions about industry "greed" and accusations of excessive pricing mainly driven by the actions of only a few players rejected by the mainstream. Every day in the news you hear about another pharmaceutical company restructuring and people losing their jobs.

What is different now? Why have the media, politicians, healthcare professionals, administrators, and, most importantly, patients turned on an industry that focuses on developing products that save lives? Why is everyone talking about the disruption of the industry? Why is the industry struggling yet still finding it challenging to rethink its business model? Who "moved its cheese?"

The U.S. healthcare industry is in turmoil, and the biopharmaceutical industry is right in the center of that storm. The industry's products are viewed as being too expensive and out of touch with what typical patients can afford, and its contributions to significant advances in health are overlooked. No value is placed on the tremendous investment made in understanding disease, nor is the cost of failures acknowledged. Marketing practices are often viewed as being misleading or worse. Furthermore, given that the industry still derives almost 50% of its global revenues from the United States, any disruption in the U.S. market has a ripple effect on the sustainability of its profits globally. How can the industry respond?

Why do some companies manage to find their way, and others stumble or even perish in such times? How does the history of the evolution of companies and industries, and the capabilities and cultures developed along the way, become enablers of or barriers to the future? How can companies proactively set up for success?

The popular, almost clichéd, answer is innovation. Everyone is writing about it. Intrinsically, we get it. It has brought us to where we are as companies, as an industry. It has contributed fundamentally to the development of the human race; and it is what will drive our future as a species. But isn't this a paradox? An industry known for innovation continues to rely on its old innovation engine based almost exclusively on discovering and developing biopharmaceuticals and no longer seems capable of innovating beyond that narrow focus to find new drivers of growth. In our view, the industry needs to fundamentally redefine innovation across a much broader spectrum of healthcare and in doing so discover new engines of growth.

Circa 2013 Jeff Huth, a senior leader at the U.S. affiliate of a top 20 global biopharmaceutical company, hired Ruchin Kansal from the world of management consulting to help prepare a historically successful organization to face the fast-changing market. The journey started with a single innovation experiment to see if the company could begin to change elements of its approach to development and commercialization through a new model grounded in co-creation with end users and payers of products. Co-funded incubators were established with customers who historically were viewed primarily as transactional partners. Initiatives were launched ranging from co-creation of outcomes research and building capabilities to identify unmet needs in patient populations, to development of healthcare solutions beyond the biopharmaceutical products that address those needs.

From there, under Ruchin's leadership, the journey included setting up additional new capabilities—in areas of digital health, patient engagement throughout the product life cycle, all the way to exploring new businesses that could be launched by leveraging core competencies of a biopharmaceutical company. These initiatives went beyond the traditional, product-focused definition of innovation in the life sciences industry.

Along the way, as has increasingly become the norm in the industry due to the changing market and pressures on both the top and bottom lines, the company went through an extensive internal transformation impacting just about every aspect of the business. In our view, there is no time more critical than during periods of dramatic change to scale and mature new ways of doing business. Such periods typically push and challenge leadership and culture to the limit. At a time that demands an unrelenting focus on uncovering new ways of working—doing things differently and doing different things—the counter pressures to preserve and support the status quo often seems to prevail.

Upon broader examination, this theme is all too common across companies in the industry. Industry leadership recognizes its business model is challenged and under continuous pressure to deliver higher margins. Consequently, almost every company has launched various initiatives focused on business transformation. The workforce in the industry has come to realize that it has to live with the constant change in organizational structure, reporting relationships, and role definitions. Most companies have also instituted innovation programs and teams. However, as you talk to leaders in charge of these efforts, you almost always hear frustration related to unclear focus, constantly changing priorities, and underinvestment because the case for changing the approach to innovation has not been made clear.

This book reflects our ambition to capture critical lessons learned through our experience in setting up innovation capabilities at our previous employer, combined with broader examination of the state of the industry, which could shape the future growth engines that go beyond monetization of the traditional biopharmaceutical product. In our view, incumbent industry players, innovators once responsible for some of the most significant advances in medical care the human race has seen, have become overly confident in what made them successful in the past. Blinded by their historical success as participants in a Unicorn Industry, they have created internal and external barriers that have inadvertently restricted their source of innovation to the biopharmaceutical product itself. As market pressures constrain their ability to sustain the underlying business model, they have largely ignored the massive environmental change taking place that can disrupt the value of their core innovation model. They have taken a narrow view of innovation focused on relatively minor modifications to their current business model while trying to maintain profitability, rather than increasing investment on identifying new sources of innovation for growth and sustained viability. Customers are bearing the burden of this institutionalized reluctance or inability to change by paying higher prices for at times incremental innovation that manifests itself in the form of another pill.

Our position is that failure to take dramatic action now will result in a slow demise or displacement of the biopharmaceutical industry's place in the healthcare value chain by disrupters from outside the industry and disappearance of many companies in the sector. This possibility has consequences far beyond the industry itself as the uncertainty associated with this market dynamic threatens the continued evolution in medical advances that we have come to take for granted in modern society. We introduce a future industry sub-sector, Smart integrated Medicine or S[i]M, for incumbents and new entrants to be relevant in the rapidly evolving hybrid human existence in the Cartesian physical space and cyberspace, especially given the emerging generational shifts.

In the sections that follow, we examine the reasons behind the pending demise of the unicorn business model of the biopharmaceutical industry based on our experience supplemented with perspectives gathered from other senior executives across several healthcare industry sectors. We propose that broadening the definition, sources, and enablers of innovation beyond the biopharmaceutical product is going to be critical for the long-term continued viability of incumbent companies, and the industry itself. We explore why, despite relatively healthy balance sheets and margins available in the near term, the industry struggles to overcome perceived capability and cultural barriers to investing in the diversification of its sources of innovation beyond the biopharmaceutical product, or chooses not to do so.

We introduce the 80-80 Rule—"being 80% confident that you will only be 80% right the first time should feel normal"—as a standard for redefining innovation and as a platform to reignite the growth engines of the biopharmaceutical industry. The 80-80 Rule advocates the underlying theme of "fit for purpose" that must be adopted by the industry as it re-examines its approach to innovating beyond traditional drug discovery and development. It emphasizes speed and the willingness to embrace a degree of uncertainty in thinking more broadly about how to define innovation.

Why do we care? Because having been inside, we know that the industry has the in-depth scientific knowledge and commercial expertise to develop meaningful solutions that go beyond traditional synthetic chemistry or biological molecule-based products if it chooses to. Because we have brilliant, well-meaning friends employed by the industry; employees who want to do good. We know many colleagues who feel constrained by the industry's focus on sustaining the status quo business model versus creating new opportunities for growth. We have friends that have seen jobs disappear due to the industry's continued consolidation as a result. We are concerned by cost inefficiencies of the current state of affairs and frustrated by the knowledge that the industry can push itself to enable a human existence grounded in good health if it chooses to. We are troubled by the current societal trust deficit; even though created by only a few bad players, it casts a dark shadow across the entire industry and will contribute to its ultimate disruption. Ironically, some of the same conditions that gave rise to this Unicorn Industry are still at work. However, this time, a simultaneous confluence of declining productivity in traditional biopharmaceutical-focused product innovation, unsustainable healthcare costs, and evolving regulatory landscape and potential disruption from outside will cause it to unravel.

We are confident that the experiences discussed here while analyzing the innovation challenge within the incumbent biopharmaceutical industry will sound familiar across most industries. Our reflections on the building blocks for reigniting innovation and transformation, how to build new capabilities, and how to drive culture change apply to any industry looking to stay relevant as the market and broader environment around it evolve.

Acknowledgments

A book is typically a story of an idea, a philosophy, or the expression of a point of view. It is a product of many people, influences, and experiences that shape authors' thinking over time. While all of us have at least one book inside our hearts and minds, only some of us are fortunate that we get to write it and get published. We want to thank our editor, Kristine Mednansky at Taylor & Francis Group, for providing us with the opportunity!

We are grateful for many experiences in our life, and for the many people who shaped our thinking along the way, that led us to become first-time authors. In particular, we would like to thank the people who contributed to the development of the manuscript. These include Michael J. Dowling, President and Chief Executive Officer, Northwell Health; Amy C. Edmondson, the Novartis Professor of Leadership and Management at the Harvard Business School; Dr. Z. Colette Edwards, Managing Editor of the *Wharton Healthcare Quarterly*, the journal of the Wharton Health Care Management Alumni Association; Dr. David Feinberg, President and Chief Executive Officer, Geisinger; Dr. William Fleming, President, Healthcare Services, Humana; Paul Fonteyne, Country Managing Director, Boehringer Ingelheim U.S.; Kurt Graves, Chief Executive Officer, Intarcia Therapeutics; Joseph La Barge, Chief Legal Officer, Spark Therapeutics; Dan Leonard, President, National Pharmaceutical

Council; Blasine Penkowski, Chief Strategic Customer Officer, Janssen North America; Dr. David Rhew, Chief Medical Officer and Head of Healthcare and Fitness, Samsung Electronics America; Donald Sawyer, Senior Vice President, Market Access and General Manager, US Established Products, Bayer; Alain Serhan, Life Sciences Leader, Egon Zehnder; Robert Spurr, Vice President, Patient Access/Health Policy, Novartis; Dr. Marcus Wilson, President, HealthCore; and Ed Yu, Chairman, Vascular Cures and retired Partner, Strategy & (PwC).

We thank Lisa Bodell, CEO of future**think** and best-selling author of *Why Simple Wins* and *Kill the Company* for writing the Foreword. Lisa is a leading authority on the subject of innovation, and an inspiration to many emerging innovators.

We thank various employers, customers, and partners that shaped our understanding of the biopharmaceutical industry, and colleagues with whom we learned and had good times along the way. In particular, we would like to thank the Boehringer Ingelheim leadership and colleagues who had the foresight to enable and support our initiatives related to establishing the innovation agenda, approach, and organizational structure for its U.S. affiliate.

We would like to thank Dr. David Memel, Rick Edmunds, and Elizabeth Powers for serving as thought partners in early experiments on the topics of innovation at Boehringer Ingelheim. We would like to thank Emily Adams for her insight into how to approach publishers and being the critical eye that helped crystallize our ideas and make them relevant as a book, and Dr. Rick Heaslip for helping us understand the publishing process through the eyes of his first-time author/ publishing experience. We thank Dr. Robin Foldsey for lending us the benefit of his extensive life sciences and pharma experience through support and coaching along the way.

Last but not least, we want to thank Hanna Tamsalu-Orlova for developing the illustrations that helped bring concepts to life, and Jane Symonds for an independent editorial reading of the manuscript. We also would like to thank Starbucks at Mill

Plain Road in Danbury for becoming our weekly office where we deliberated and developed the project.

I (Ruchin) would like to dedicate this book to my father, Subodh, and my mother, Sudha. I would like to thank my wife, Gunjan, for being my life partner, for always believing in me, and for never giving up on the idea that I could write a book, even though she remains amused by the fact that I can write! Thanks to my son, Neil, for actually reading an early draft and questioning me on the thesis of the book; and my brother, Sachin, who always stands by me. Thanks to Puja Gupta, Neil Jain, and Purav Gandhi for reading the first drafts and providing feedback and critique. Thank you to Jeff, my partner, and mentor—who gave me the chance to experiment with innovation, learned with me along the way, and agreed to work on this book project with me; to Cindy Tomich, who many years ago planted the seed for the idea that I should write a book; and lastly, to Roo, who sat by my desk keeping me company during brief moments of lucidity I had that helped shape the concepts in the book.

I (Jeff) would like to thank my wife, Marie, for her support and for tolerating the mess at the kitchen table for several months, and my adult children, Allison and Megan, for their encouragement throughout the process. I would like to reciprocate in thanking my co-author, Ruchin, for developing the initial concept for this effort and persistence in keeping us on track during the writing process.

Lastly, we would like to acknowledge you, the readers. First, for buying the book and thereby confirming the validity of its content. Secondly, and more importantly, we hope that reading this book will encourage you to think about embracing the 80-80 Rule, doing things differently, and doing different things as a way to innovate and succeed in your work, and in your life.

The 80-80 Rule

Not taking chances is not an option.

"Being 80% confident that you will only be 80% right the first time should feel normal."

- If you are 100% confident, you are not looking for blind-spots. This attitude borders on arrogance.
- If you wait to be 100% confident, it probably means that someone else may have already capitalized on your idea because you spent too much time in the quest for perfection.
- And if you are 100% right the first time, it is pure chance, not an act of genius.

It is a pretty safe bet that all of our readers are familiar with the Pareto principle (also known as the 80/20 rule), which states that, for many events, roughly 80% of the effects come from 20% of the causes. We would like to introduce the 80-80 Rule governing how to adjust thinking and behavior when the urgency to innovate is evident: "Being 80% confident that you will only be 80% right the first time should feel normal." The 80-80 Rule should not be interpreted as a statistical methodology for predicting success in business endeavors; instead, it is intended to reflect a required philosophical shift toward challenging the status quo in just about every aspect of business innovation.

In our view, the one quality that makes innovators successful is that they resist the temptation of always trying to be 100% right every time. Instead, they have an overarching vision, and they are not afraid to make mistakes along the way toward achieving that vision.

In corporate environments, especially where the incumbent has been successful and an industry leader for long periods of time, the focus becomes building a replicable machine that runs the core business over and over again efficiently. Risk taking is minimized and replaced by standard operating procedures, efficiency overrules experimentation, pre-defined metrics drive performance, and incentives are tied to current financial returns. The spirit of innovation, taking risks, experimenting—the very characteristics that made the incumbent successful in the first place—are often lost.

Continuing to think beyond the status quo of the core business to transform or disrupt it requires a mindful culture, and a deliberate focus and effort. It should allow individuals within organizations to realize how existing strengths can be applied to discover new paths and businesses of the future. Intentional innovation, understanding that fast failure coupled with objective review can itself be a relevant metric, and being 80% confident that initially any solution will only be 80% right is a good thing. The biopharmaceutical industry is very comfortable with the risk and failure rate inherent in the discovery and development of its current products. However, it struggles to adopt a similar risk-based philosophy when thinking about a broader definition of innovation which we believe is essential for long-term viability. The 80-80 Rule intends to rekindle that spirit of innovation by making the discomfort and conflict that comes with challenging the status quo feel normal again.

We are, however, not advocating that risk taking or experimentation should be an unstructured exercise. If you are 100% confident that every experiment undertaken will yield positive results, you are not being pragmatic and looking for blind-spots. This attitude borders on arrogance. At the same time, if you wait to be 100% certain before moving to the next step, it probably means that someone else may have already capitalized on your idea because you spent too much time in the quest for perfection. Also know that if you are 100% right the first time, it is pure chance, not an act of genius.

The 80-80 Rule means having the courage to explore unknown paths, recognizing that there will be failure along the way. It is only through exploration and experimentation that the new is discovered, that innovation becomes real. In this book, we examine how the 80-80 Rule can create the shift so urgently needed by the biopharmaceutical industry to find its way back to its former glory.

REDEFINING
INNOVATION

Chapter 1

Rise of a Unicorn Industry

"History cannot give us a program for the future, but it can give us a fuller understanding of ourselves, and of our common humanity, so we can better face the future."

Robert Penn Warren

The birth of a Unicorn Industry.

Unintended Consequences of Disconnected Choices

u · ni · corn
noun
noun: **unicorn**; *plural noun:* **unicorns**

1. *a mythical animal typically represented as a horse with a single straight horn projecting from its forehead. a heraldic representation of a unicorn, with a twisted horn, a deer's feet, a goat's beard, and a lion's tail.*

2. *a start-up company valued at more than a billion dollars, typically in the software or technology sector.*[1]

In literature, the term unicorn is typically used to refer to something mythical that does not exist. It was first used by Aileen Lee, the founder of Cowboy Ventures, to describe tech start-ups that achieve a $1 billion market valuation, either through private or public investment. Typically, these unicorns are grounded in innovation—they plug an unmet need looking for a solution or occasionally create a solution that fills a need even before it is recognized. However, seldom does one hear about "Unicorn Industries."

We define "Unicorn Industries" as sectors in which every company in the industry has the potential to achieve a billion dollars in sales (not just valuation), often defying the logic of supply and demand, not only because they have a highly innovative offering that fills an unmet market need, but because the business model of the industry is such that it almost guarantees that outcome—at least historically.

The story of the biopharmaceutical industry in the United States is a story of a Unicorn Industry. The underpinnings that would make it so were firmly in place by the early 1990s given an unusual confluence of three factors:

- A peak in the industry's product innovation output given the investments made after the Second World War;
- An uptick in reimbursement rates driven by employer-sponsored insurance and concurrent maturity of the industry's physician-focused commercial model that emerged in response to the 1951 Durham-Humphrey amendment[2] to regulations governing the Food and Drug Administration (FDA); and
- A relatively stable and in some cases an extended period of market exclusivity granted by the Drug Price Competition and Patent Term Restoration Act of 1984, commonly known as the Hatch–Waxman Act.

These factors gave rise to a U.S.-centric Unicorn Industry where the business model would support an average profit margin of 21% year after year, making it the most profitable of all industries even today.[3]

It's not a story of a single person's vision. It's a story of disconnected actions that collectively had an unforeseen long-term consequence. It's a story of an industry that has defied business and economic conventions and resisted many forces that pressure companies in other industry sectors to evolve or face obsolescence rapidly. It's a story of the Unicorn Industry that created blockbusters—products that would generate more than 1 billion dollars in revenue year after year utilizing the industry's unique business model. Lipitor, indicated for lowering "bad" cholesterol, generated USD 7.7 billion in U.S. sales in 2011. Plavix, prescribed for preventing clots and heart attacks: USD 6.8 billion. In 2016, Humira, prescribed for various arthritic conditions, was projected to bring in USD 15.7 billion.

However, the industry is facing strong headwinds as it increasingly sees its historical product value proposition and profit model challenged as healthcare costs continue to escalate to unsustainable levels. To better understand the biopharmaceutical industry of today, we start with a brief history to provide a perspective on how the confluence of seemingly unrelated events led to the emergence of the Unicorn. We can then begin to understand why there is such a crisis of innovation in the industry today and gaps in its ability to rethink itself. We can then start to grasp why successful industry participants are ignoring the signals of the industry's demise demonstrated by an absence of immediate, meaningful action, and why there is a platform to identify, mature and scale new capabilities in areas of innovation that go beyond the biopharmaceutical product itself to drive future growth.

The Western Biopharmaceutical Industry Takes Shape

It is only in the last 150 years that the field of western medicine has rapidly become a scientific enterprise delivering significant advances in the understanding of human biology translated into both diagnostics and treatments. Before that, globally, most ailments were treated by products based on a variety of natural herbs, spices, and their blends created by druids, healers, elders, and vaidyas trained through the art of observation as opposed to science. While Chinese traditional medicine, Unani medicine from the Middle East, and Ayurveda from India have a long history, they have come up short in their ability to help manage diseases and improve human life as much as advances in modern western medicine have done.

The modern western biopharmaceutical industry started to take shape in the early 1800s. As the industrial revolution took hold, Germany, Switzerland, the United Kingdom, and the United States saw the emergence of chemical companies beginning to synthesize compounds for treating human ailments (Figure 1.1). This period saw the entry of the term "chemists" in the U.K. and "pharmacist" or "druggist" into the lexicon of several countries to describe the professional in

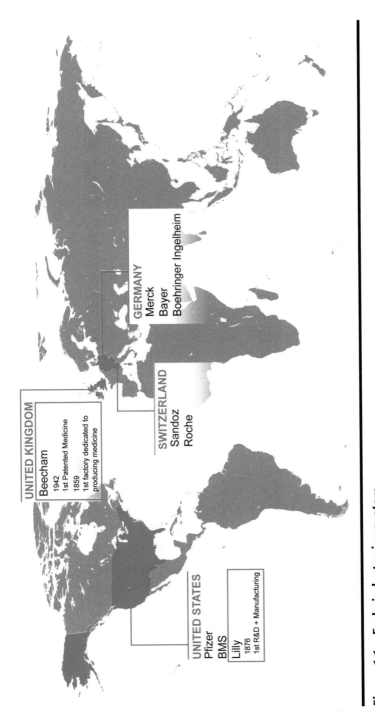

Figure 1.1 Early industry innovators.

today's Pharmacy industry. This synergy between industrial chemicals and pharmaceuticals persisted into the twentieth century, with many large companies having both chemicals and pharmaceutical divisions.

In Germany, Merck, Bayer, and Boehringer Ingelheim were early pioneers. Merck, with its origin as an apothecary, can attribute its initial growth to the commercial production of morphine in 1827 to manage pain. Bayer was formed in 1863 to manufacture and sell synthetic dyestuffs to the textile industry, and developed Aspirin in 1899 based on chemical modification of salicylic acid, a natural remedy historically extracted from willow bark and other plants for the treatment of pain, fever, and inflammation. Boehringer Ingelheim was founded in 1885 initially producing tartaric and lactic acid from by-products of local wineries of the Rhine valley for use by pharmacies and dye manufacturers. It launched its first pharmaceutical product—an analgesic called Laudanon— in 1912. Switzerland gave rise to Sandoz and Roche. In the U.K., in 1842, Thomas Beecham, a shepherd who sold herbal remedies on the side, started selling Beecham's Pills as a laxative. This activity was the origin (post multiple mergers) of the company we know today as GlaxoSmithKline. In the United States, Pfizer was founded in 1849 as a manufacturer of fine chemicals. Their first therapeutic product was Antonin, an anti-parasitic that found a market due to rampant intestinal infection in nineteenth century America. Squibb Corporation and Bristol Myers Corporation (started as Clinton Pharmaceuticals) followed similar patterns.

The concept of patent medicines was introduced in England in the 1600s and leveraged extensively in the late nineteenth and early twentieth centuries by the then-nascent pharmaceutical industry to drive its early growth. Medicine could be patented as long as it was original. Further, given the non-specific nature of the law, as long as a remedy or a potion had a unique name, it was patented. What is interesting is that the basis for the patent at this time was merely an advertising designation often linked to a royal endorsement, without regard to safety or efficacy properties of the suggested medication. Products were sold without a prescription and heavily promoted as medical panaceas often with royal support, emphasizing exotic ingredients, and testimonials from celebrities or purported experts devoid of documented scientific evidence in the claims. One can recognize this as the origins of current branding and advertising of pharmaceutical products.[4,5,6] It is estimated that by 1900, 72% of drugs sold were patent medicines.[7]

While the availability of patent medicine was widespread, the early foundation of a more structured scientific research-based drug discovery enterprise was also being laid. Eli Lilly & Company, incorporated in 1881, differentiated itself via a focus on prescription (not patent) medicines. Colonel Eli Lilly is considered the pioneer of the modern "end to end" pharmaceutical company by bringing drug research & development (R&D) and manufacturing under the same banner at the company bearing his name today. Over time, the R&D function became the innovation engine of the biopharmaceutical industry and remains so today.

Further, the progressive era of journalism from 1890 to 1910 gave rise to challenges to some of the patent medicine claims with the appearance of published reports of addiction, death, and other side effects of these medicines. In response, in 1906, the U.S. government passed the Pure Food and Drug Act requiring suppliers to label 11 dangerous elements—alcohol, opium, and stimulants among others—present in these medicines (Figure 1.2). This legislation subsequently led to the removal of such ingredients from medications.[8] It also prohibited "false and misleading" statements on product labels—however, with limited success in enforcement.[9] More importantly, in our view, this Act paved the foundation of the modern western prescription medicine industry and marked the beginning of the journey towards industry regulation.

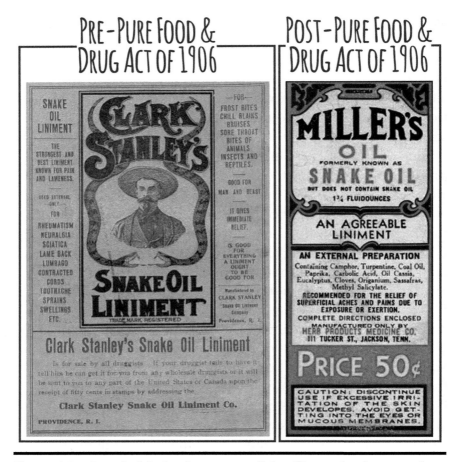

Figure 1.2 Sample labels of patent medicine illustrating impact of Pure Food and Drug Act (1906) requirement to list ingredients.

World War I slowed the development of the still-nascent modern pharmaceutical industry especially in Europe. The industry remained highly fragmented and loosely regulated. At the same time, the industry produced several scientific breakthroughs, including the development of insulin in 1921 for treatment of diabetes, and of penicillin in 1928 to treat bacterial infections.

Then, in 1937 more than 100 people died after ingesting the liquid formulation of Sulfanilamide (used to treat streptococcal infections) manufactured by S.E. Massengill Company of Tennessee. While Sulfanilamide by itself was effective for treating various conditions ranging from gonorrhea to a sore throat, the cause of death was diethylene glycol present in the formulation. People were looking for an easy-to-administer formulation, and diethylene glycol was used as a solvent to create an elixir, however, it was never tested for safety before inclusion in a medicinal product introduced into the market. Sadly, at the time there was a lack of regulations under which to penalize the company, and that subsequently led to public demand for the same. This outcry and other similar events resulted in the passage of the Federal Food, Drug, and Cosmetics Act of 1938 (FDCA). For the first time, the regulation required proof of safety of medicines before they could be sold. The FDA had 60 days to review the data provided on safety studies. Interestingly, however, if the FDA did not respond within that period, the company could then proceed with the market introduction of the product.[10]

That said, this was the first significant industry regulation that further strengthened the foundation of the modern biopharmaceutical industry. With the passage of the act, a clear signal was sent that human safety is of prime importance and non-negotiable. The law was applied to synthetic products being developed and sold as prescription medicines, not to traditional home remedies or those available for example through the fields of Ayurveda or Chinese Traditional Medicine. As a result, we can concur that this was the time when the real divergence between the practice of traditional versus modern medicine started. With the application of scientific rigor and regulatory framework focused on human safety, the western biopharmaceutical industry started to become the harbinger of medical care across the world.

Globally, the industry primarily operated on a Business to Consumer (B2C) business model during this period. Patients would pay out of pocket for any healthcare services or medicines received. Additionally, medical schools had started to mature in training healthcare workers, and physicians began to gain prestige as professionals. They assumed the role of scientific experts influencing the prescription of medication. However, prescribing privilege was not limited to just the physicians. Chemists working at apothecaries and pharmacies were still a trusted source of product choice.

The Golden Era

The period from 1940 to the 1980s can be considered the golden age of synthetic chemistry in the biopharmaceutical industry. At the end of World War II, both the National Health Service (NHS) in the U.K. and the Office of Science & Research Development (OSRD), the precursor of the National Institutes of Health (NIH), in the United States invested heavily in private partnerships to drive the pharmaceutical research enterprise. In the United States alone, investment in medical and scientific research grew from $161 million in 1950 to over $2.5 billion in 1968.[11] Although such investments initially focused on the large-scale production of penicillin, the industrialization of pharmaceutical R&D quickly resulted in multiple other innovations coming to market—anti-infectives such as Terramycin, the birth control pill, the polio vaccine, ACE inhibitors, valium, paracetamol, ibuprofen, and cancer drugs, to name a few.

Synthetic chemistry was the first real technological innovation of the pharmaceutical industry that matured during this time and scaled to become the basis for discovery of multiple chronic-disease-focused prescription products. Consider the power of human enterprise that has developed a precise ability to alter and combine synthetic modifications of various naturally occurring substances, compounds generated through random screening of large chemical libraries or specific receptor agonists/antagonists, all contributing to the formation of new compounds. These new ones could precisely target and modify the natural biological processes causing disease in the human body!

While synthetic chemistry-based products dominated the so-called Golden Era, it was also during this period that research into Deoxyribonucleic Acid (DNA) as the basic building block of molecular biology carrying genetic instructions for growth, development, functioning, and reproduction of living organisms emerged. Classified as biotechnology, it became the next technological innovation adopted by the industry during the latter part of this period. Akin to synthetic chemistry where chemical processes are used to create new compounds, biotechnology focuses on harnessing and/or modifying naturally occurring proteins and antibodies to influence physiological processes of mammalian cells and microorganisms that cause disease. In 1982, the first biotech product, human insulin derived from genetically modified bacteria developed by Genentech and Eli Lilly was approved by the FDA. By the end of the 1980s, the multiple products derived from biotechnology were approved by the FDA and other regulatory authorities and commercialized. Northern California became the hotbed of biotech revolution, and companies such as Amgen, Chiron, and others evolved as early innovators of biologics. Silicon Valley had a new neighbor, the Biotech Bay.

These technological innovations—think of them as the core programming languages of the biopharmaceutical industry—allowed rapid development of innovative biopharmaceutical products responsible for the management of most chronic and many specialty, rare, and orphan diseases, including oncology and immunology. Investments poured in, given the promise of financial returns attained by solving for rampant unmet needs in human health.

While the Golden Era from the 1940s to the 1980s was a period of rapid innovation and associated profits, it also saw the emergence of further regulation to ensure the protection of the patient/consumer. In 1951, Senator Hubert H. Humphrey Jr.

and Representative Carl Durham representing North Carolina proposed the Durham-Humphrey amendment[12] to statutes governing the FDA. The amendment created a clear distinction between products requiring a prescription and therefore dispensed under the supervision of a health practitioner (sometimes called behind the counter products), versus those that did not fall into that category and what we now call Over the Counter (OTC) products. The initial goal was to ensure that any drug that could be habit-forming or potentially harmful could only be prescribed by a licensed practitioner—primarily physicians—and in the process, pharmacists lost the power to dispense such products in the absence of a physician-initiated prescription. This amendment can be linked to the elevation of physicians as essential intermediaries in the delivery of care from a regulatory perspective and consequently the emergence of the physician-focused commercial model in the United States. Given that prescribing privileges were limited to licensed physicians, biopharmaceutical companies started to build a selling model focused on providing extensive information on the clinical profile of biopharmaceutical products to the level that the practice came to be known as "detailing" the physicians. Key Opinion Leaders (KOLs), accomplished physicians in their fields of practice usually affiliated with Academic Medical Centers, became important influencers of prescribing behavior. Wildly successful for an extended period in driving product uptake in the market, this physician-focused commercial model has been the mainstay of the biopharmaceutical industry in the United States and many other countries until very recently.

What is important to note is that outside the United States regulation has not limited prescribing authority only to physicians. In many parts of the developed world, licensed pharmacists (e.g., in the U.K. and some European countries) have the authorization to dispense so-called behind the counter medications that are prescription-only in the United States.

In most of the developing world, one is still able to walk into the local pharmacy and purchase most common prescription products (including antibiotics) based on the advice of the chemist or based on institutional knowledge of family and friends. Lately, even in the United States, some states are considering broadening varying levels of pharmacy (and other allied health professionals) prescribing authority to address the growing shortage of primary care physicians.

As can often occur during periods of rapid and sometimes uncontrolled growth in sectors, the industry was impacted by a major event in the form of the thalidomide scandal in 1961 which once again shaped the state of the pharmaceutical industry. The general literature on the topic suggests that thalidomide, developed initially as a hypnotic but also prescribed for easing morning sickness in pregnant women, caused severe congenital abnormalities in their babies. Due to government pressure, its manufacturer, Grünenthal, reluctantly removed the drug from the markets in Germany in 1961. Despite the fact that it was not approved for sale in the United States by the FDA, Grünenthal's U.S. licensee, the William S. Merrell Company, distributed thousands of samples of the drug without appropriate warning of potential side effects in what were characterized as clinical trials (although the design and conduct of which would be viewed as questionable under today's standards).[13] Similar to the experience in Germany, women who were administered thalidomide while pregnant frequently gave birth to children with severe congenital abnormalities.

This scandal led to further updates to regulations governing the biopharmaceutical industry. In 1962 the Kefauver–Harris amendment to the 1938 Food, Drug and Cosmetics Act sponsored by U.S. Senator Estes Kefauver of Tennessee and U.S. Representative Oren Harris of Arkansas was enacted into law. Under this bill, biopharmaceutical companies were required to prove that the drugs were both safe and efficacious before commercialization. These companies were obligated to conduct specific pre-clinical tests to examine effects of potential new treatments on animals before testing for safety and efficacy in humans. Other regulations around the same time included the Declaration of Helsinki addressing ethical considerations of medical research. All regulation was geared to ensuring that pharmaceutical companies conducted Randomized Controlled Trials (RCTs) to conduct safety and effectiveness studies that the FDA had to review and approve before a product could be commercialized. The 60-day wait time limit for commercialization in the absence of FDA approval was removed. FDA approval became mandatory prior to commercialization. Further, companies were now required to follow good manufacturing practices (GMP).[14]

The regulation, while it might have felt onerous at the time given that biopharmaceutical companies had to invest in building clinical trial capabilities, ultimately led to the standardization of R&D processes and the commercialization tied to the product label (Figure 1.3[15]), further differentiating

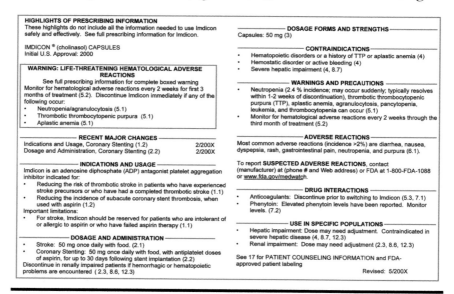

Figure 1.3   Sample label for a (fictitious) modern prescription product illustrating required elements.

the western biopharmaceutical industry from other existing suppliers of medical treatments that lagged in scientific evidence of their effectiveness. Given the heightened scrutiny of the label and regulation to restrict the use of products to approved claims, the industry now turned its focus on further refining its commercial model to highlight the approved messages to drive prescriptions. The innovation engine of the industry was now running at full steam. It granted the biopharmaceutical industry a sense of legitimacy at a level that the practices of traditional medicine have never been able to attain.

As another example of an unintended consequence, one of the most prominent barriers faced by developers of digital health solutions regarding adoption and reimbursement is the highly regulated process necessary to gain FDA approval of their scientific claims of effectiveness.

From a payment perspective, the United States, Europe, and newly independent emerging countries took radically different approaches. Most of the European countries looked at healthcare as the responsibility of the government and created single-payer systems funded by tax revenue. Newly independent, emerging nations coming out of the colonial era focused on public health initiatives to control large-scale epidemics and rampant disease. However, given the basic financial systems and budget capacities, most of the burden of paying for more routine healthcare fell on individuals and families, and this remains the case. On the other hand, the United States saw the emergence of a healthcare system that was funded by a mix of employers and government, where out-of-pocket costs for healthcare declined relatively over time.[16] General Motors became the first large company to provide health insurance to its 180,000 workers. Employers' contributions to healthcare climbed steadily after World War II and quickly evolved from a tool for competing for employees to an expectation, especially for large employers and unions. Further, in 1965, the government signed into law the Medicare and Medicaid programs, affirming the role of the state as sponsors of healthcare financing. Health insurance companies emerged as the intermediary to facilitate buying coverage for healthcare medical services and prescription products on behalf of employers and governments. While Blue Cross started selling insurance for hospital care in the 1930s, it is estimated that by the 1960s more than 700 health insurance companies were operating in the United States. The market remained highly fragmented till the 1980s; consequently, the provider market and the biopharmaceuticals market remained fragmented as well. The overall healthcare cost as a percentage of national Gross Domestic Product (GDP) was at a relatively acceptable level of 5% in the 1960s. The healthcare ecosystem, comprised of employers, government and patients as payers, insurance companies as intermediaries, and providers and biopharmaceutical manufacturers as suppliers, started to form without much foresight of the complex beast it would become in the future.

In retrospect, this period was characterized by genuine product innovation in the biopharmaceutical industry. Synthetic chemistry and biotechnology, two enabling platforms developed during this time, were the primary technologies responsible for all biopharmaceutical product innovation, which remains even today. Regulation paved the pathway to ensure that biopharmaceuticals products introduced in the market were safe and effective for human use. To further drive public safety, the Durham-Humphrey amendment established physicians as the primary mechanism to manage the risk of prescription medicine. However, while the regulation was written to enable public safety, the physician-focused commercial model that emerged as a consequence of the law provided one of the critical building blocks of the unicorn biopharmaceutical industry that matured in the 1980s and 1990s in the United States. Lastly, the loosely forming insurance-based Business to Business (B2B) healthcare system that started to emerge in this period would mature and become the third building block of the industry over the next two decades.

A "Unicorn Industry" Is in Place

Unicorn Industry Achieves Maximum Velocity

There is a term used in the automobile industry called "convergent innovation." It refers to the notion that cars are fundamentally indistinguishable from each other as a means of transportation. An Audi Q5 is very similar to a BMW X3 which is very similar to a Mercedes Benz GLC, and as a result, the battle for market leadership is grounded in marketing, pricing, and sales strategies. The latter part of the twentieth century saw convergent innovation become the norm in the biopharmaceutical industry as well.

In the 1980s, as the industry's innovation engine churned out one innovative product after another, the race to get FDA approvals intensified as the primary source of competitive advantage necessary to launch products in the market. Even generic formulations had to go through an FDA approval process similar to that for the innovator products. Further, legal battles to protect the intellectual property created in the Research & Development divisions of companies intensified to keep competitors at bay. Generic formulations of innovator products that could bring the prices of innovator products down were legally challenged during the patent protection periods accorded by law.

The FDA found itself short on resources to review and approve both innovator and generic products for market consumption. To speed up the process of bringing generics to market and provide branded product companies continued incentives to innovate, Representative Henry Waxman of California and Senator Orrin Hatch of Utah sponsored the Drug Price Competition and Patent Term Restoration Act in 1984, commonly known as the Hatch–Waxman Act. On the one hand, the act accelerated the process of bringing generic pharmaceutical products to market through a documented, transparent abbreviated new drug application (ANDA)— helping consumers gain access to cheaper versions of innovator products meeting a uniform set of standards. On the other hand, as the FDA approval process became costlier and more time-consuming for innovator products, the act granted five years of market exclusivity to compensate for the time spent in the regulated development and approval process. An additional provision was an automatic delay of 30 months to launch a generic version if the patent owner challenged the generic manufacturer for patent infringement.

At the same time, the B2B healthcare ecosystem that had started to take shape in the previous decade began to mature. With increasing demand for healthcare products and services linked to an aging population and availability of innovations in the diagnostic, therapeutic, and surgical areas, the share of healthcare as a percent of GDP started to increase. Insurance companies consolidated to yield greater purchasing power. Group Purchasing Organizations (GPOs) matured as consolidators of purchasing power for hospital supplies. Pharmacy benefit managers (PBMs) emerged to consolidate the purchasing power for pharmaceuticals on behalf of employer and insurance company clients, and pharmaceutical companies started to merge to "buy" product innovation, maintain critical mass in marketing strength, and protect pricing power.

In economics, the principle of supply and demand typically governs the ability to price products and services, and the pricing power fluctuates based on the number of suppliers and users. The higher the number on both sides, the higher the negotiating power, and as a result, the prices are typically lower. The lower the number on both sides, the smaller the negotiating power, resulting in higher prices. Also, a single buyer can constrain the price of suppliers more efficiently than multiple buyers. Given that various players emerged to facilitate the employer and government-funded healthcare system in the United States, the system never became fully market efficient. While intermediaries like insurance companies, Group Purchasing Organizations, and Pharmacy Benefit Managers applied pricing pressure, given the relative demand inelasticity of healthcare in a country where healthcare is considered a right, providers and pharmaceutical companies still found it possible to continue to increase prices at a healthy rate. As a result, the total cost of the healthcare system comprised of various intermediaries and suppliers continued to grow and was passed on to employers and governments, thereby increasing premiums.

In 1993, the employer costs to cover pharmaceuticals through insurance programs became higher than out-of-pocket costs, and then accelerated significantly as shown in Figure 1.4.[17] According to the National Center for Biotechnology Information (NCBI), "Out-of-pocket payments

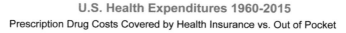

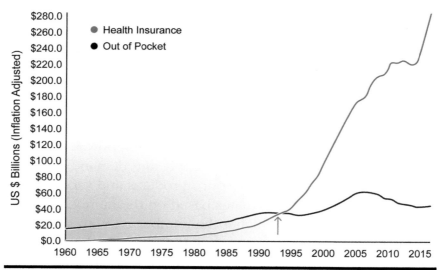

Figure 1.4 Divergence in prescription drug costs covered by health insurance versus out-of-pocket accelerates in 1993.

increased by an annual average of just over 5% while third-party payments increased by over 17% annually."[18] By this time, the biopharmaceutical industry had perfected its commercial model that emerged in the previous decades. It enabled the industry to significantly increase its revenue from 1995 to 2005 (Figure 1.5[19]), leveraging the fact that healthcare was now primarily paid for by employers and governments and price transparency and controls were non-existent. The revenue growth has since moderated on an annual basis.

Product monopolies were born and the concept of a blockbuster product—a biopharmaceutical product that could generate greater than USD one billion in revenues per year—came into vogue. While Zantac, prescribed for heartburn, is considered the first blockbuster drug that achieved the status in the mid-1980s, 1995 is the first year when 21 drugs reached blockbuster status.[20] Zoloft, Lipitor, and Viagra all launched during this time and were some of the earliest blockbusters.

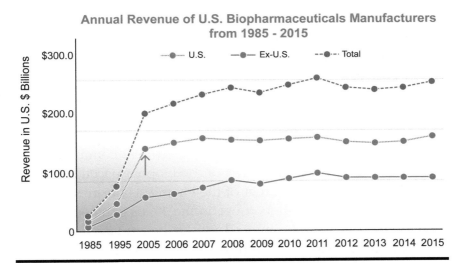

Figure 1.5   Annual revenues of U.S. biopharmaceutical industry rise between 1995 and 2005, driven by health insurance-based reimbursement.

Sales & Marketing functions that found their roots in the advertising days of patent medicines in the 1800s and further developed to drive physician-focused promotion after the Durham-Humphrey act mandated it, matured as the primary drivers of the industry. For the first time, marketing and sales leaders in the industry versus R&D scientists started to be the face of products' success, which was measured in commercial terms. Blockbuster status of drugs was attributed as much to the leaders responsible for marketing and sales as to the underlying scientific innovation.

Also, given the large markets in chronic diseases, the available advantage of market exclusivity granted by the Hatch–Waxman Act, and increasing pricing power due to demand inelasticity driven by fragmented payment models, the race to be first to market with true patented innovative product intensified. It can be argued that over the next two decades, such patent protection allowed the biopharmaceutical industry to create virtual product monopolies, with intensifying legal defense of patents to keep competition at bay.

On the revenue side, a wave of innovative products coupled with the ability to increase prices created a potent combination. Regarding costs, companies found the sweet spot regarding the investment allocation between R&D and marketing and sales, with R&D investment averaging about 20% of net sales and marketing and sales investment averaging 40%. This model allowed the industry to generate 16%–24% profit margins, which became the expectation of the investment community. Given that the investment returns of the biopharmaceutical business started to exceed that of the chemicals businesses where the industry found its roots, in the 1990s conglomerates such as Hoechst, Ciba-Geigy, and Sandoz began to spin off their pharmaceutical business units. Aventis was a spin-off from Hoechst subsequently acquired by Sanofi to become Sanofi-Aventis. Novartis was formed from the merger of divested pharma businesses from Ciba-Geigy and Sandoz. AstraZeneca was formed by a merger of the Swedish company Astra AB with the British company Zeneca itself originally established as a demerger from Imperial Chemical Industries (ICI).[21]

The unique combination of regulation and high reimbursement rates afforded by insurance-based payment systems made the United States the most profitable market for the biopharmaceutical industry influenced by:

- Growth in the industry's innovation output which peaked in 1997 with the approval of 55 new molecular entities (and has since declined, which we will discuss later);
- The maturity of its commercial model that emerged in response to the Durham-Humphrey amendment; and
- A relatively extended period of market exclusivity granted by the Hatch–Waxman Act.

The industry now focused its attention on maintaining profit margins to satisfy the investment community. In the face of a business model which could deliver high financial returns, "me too" products characterized by incremental innovation which could be defended in court based on strong patent laws became the norm. Legal battles to protect patents intensified to maximize the profit potential of biopharmaceutical products during periods of market exclusivity.

Based on these factors, the unicorn business model of the pharmaceutical industry was firmly in place. The "Unicorn Industry" would grow from introducing 21 blockbusters in 1995 to 47 in 2000 and 101 in 2005.[22] In comparison, since Bloom Energy, a green-tech company, became the first unicorn in 2009, the tech industry has produced a total of 105 unicorns between 2009 and mid-2017 in the United States.[23]

A Perspective on Global Differences in Reimbursement of Biopharmaceuticals

From a payment perspective, the developed world outside of the United States often evolved to a single-payer system to exert control on pricing of healthcare services including pharmaceuticals through the power of negotiation driven by total cost and affordability considerations consolidated under one buyer. As a result, the industry never became as profitable in the rest of the developed world as in the United States. In contrast to the situation in the United States and other developed markets, the emerging economies of the world still predominantly depended on a self-pay system, which given the principles of supply and demand and lower purchasing power, have kept the pricing and relative profitability of pharmaceutical products down. In fact, in India, my (Ruchin's) parents can call the local pharmacist for the medicines they need, and it is delivered to their home. Further, they can even return unused medication in the original packaging within six months of purchase for a full refund.

Given the market dynamics described, nations with strong patent laws and single-payer systems may have benefited the most from the biopharmaceutical industry's innovation—as they had access to most of the latest innovation at low prices. There were, however, some notable exceptions. I (Jeff) lived in the U.K. during a period in which local health authorities sometimes restricted access to new medicines to people living in a community. Yet, people living in another part of the same community (sometimes literally on the other side of the street) but subject to oversight by a different health authority could get the same medication. This practice became known as post-code prescribing. The National Institute for Clinical Effectiveness (NICE) came along and implemented restrictions on new products such that everyone was uniformly denied any medical innovation that didn't meet the pre-defined cost-effectiveness hurdle. The continued availability of innovative products at lower prices in Europe and other single-payer markets may soon begin to decline as U.S.-based manufacturers, PBMs, and the U.S. federal government are starting to question why the United States should in effect "subsidize" lower prices by multi-national corporations outside the country.

Emerging economies may have benefited the least from biopharmaceutical innovation due to the limited patent protection, inability to command high prices due to the predominant self-pay models, and paying capacity. The biopharmaceutical industry has limited the launch of the latest innovative products in such countries. They typically do so after the pricing advantage available in developed markets is exhausted. Sadly, for U.S. patients, even though the innovation is readily accessible, it is often mostly incremental and comes at a high price which is reflected in a continued increase in healthcare expenditure as a percent of GDP.

Endnotes

1. Dictionary.com
2. Public Law 215, Statute 65, *An Act to Amend Sections 303 (c) and 503 (b) of the Federal Food, Drug, and Cosmetic Act, as amended.* October 26, 1951, accessed January 19, 2018, https://www.gpo.gov/fdsys/pkg/STATUTE-65/pdf/STATUTE-65-Pg648.pdf

3. Keith Speights, *"12 Big Pharma Stats That Will Blow You Away,"* July 31, 2016, accessed January 19, 2018, https://www.fool.com/investing/2016/07/31/12-big-pharma-stats-that-will-blow-you-away.aspx

4. Peggy M. Baker, *Patent Medicine: Cures and Quacks*, Pilgrim Society and Pilgrim Hall Museum; accessed January 19, 2018, http://www.pilgrimhallmuseum.org/pdf/Patent_Medicine.pdf

5. Encyclopedia.com, Thomson Gale, *"Patent Medicine,"* 1997, accessed January 19, 2018, http://www.encyclopedia.com/medicine/drugs/pharmacology/patent-medicine

6. U.S. National Library of Medicine, *"Medical Show,"* accessed January 19, 2018, https://www.nlm.nih.gov/exhibition/ephemera/medshow.html

7. Susanne White Junod Ph.D. and William Thomas Beaver, *"FDA and Clinical Drug Trials: A Short History,"* U.S. Food & Drug Administration, accessed January 19, 2018, https://www.fda.gov/AboutFDA/WhatWeDo/History/Overviews/ucm304485.htm

8. Junod et al., *"FDA and Clinical Drug Trials: A Short History."*

9. Junod et al., *"FDA and Clinical Drug Trials: A Short History."*

10. Junod et al., *"FDA and Clinical Drug Trials: A Short History."*

11. Junod et al., *"FDA and Clinical Drug Trials: A Short History."*

12. Public Law 215, Statute 65, An Act to Amend Sections 303 (c) and 503 (b) of the Federal Food, Drug, and Cosmetic Act, as amended. October 26, 1951, accessed January 19, 2018, https://www.gpo.gov/fdsys/pkg/STATUTE-65/pdf/STATUTE-65-Pg648.pdf

13. Adam Bernstein and Patricia Sullivan, "Frances Oldham Kelsey, FDA Scientist Who Kept Thalidomide off U.S. Market Dies at 101" *The Washington Post,* August 7, 2015.

14. Junod et al., *"FDA and Clinical Drug Trials: A Short History."*

15. Mary E. Kremzner, Steven F. Osborne, *"An Introduction to the Improved FDA Drug Labeling,"* Center for Drug Evaluation & Research, U.S. Food & Drug Administration, Page 23, accessed January 19, 2018, https://www.fda.gov/downloads/training/forhealthprofessionals/ucm090796.pdf

16. CMS.gov, Aaron C. Catlin and Cathy A. Cowan, *"History of Health Spending in the United States, 1960–2013,"* November 19, 2015, accessed January 19, 2018, https://www.cms.gov/Research-Statistics-Data-and-Systems/Statistics-Trends-and-Reports/NationalHealthExpendData/Downloads/HistoricalNHEPaper.pdf

17. Peterson-Kaiser Health System Tracker, *"Health Spending Explorer, Trends by Source of Funds,"* accessed January 19, 2018, https://www.healthsystemtracker.org/interactive/?display=U.S.%2520%2524%2520Billions%2520-%2520Inflation%2520Adjusted&service=Prescription%2520Drug&source=Health%2520Insurance%252COut%2520of%2520Pocket&tab=1

18. David K. Baugh, M.A., Penelope L. Pine, Steve Blackwell, Ph.D., J.D., R.Ph., and Gary Ciborowski, M.A., "Medicaid Prescription Drug Spending in the 1990s: A Decade of Change," *Health Care Finance Review*, v.25(3); Spring 2004, PMC4194863.

19. Statista, *"U.S. Pharmaceutical Industry—Domestic and Abroad Revenue 1975–2015,"* accessed January 19, 2018, https://www.statista.com/statistics/275560/domestic-and-international-revenue-of-the-us-pharmaceutical-industry/

20. L.E.K. Consulting, "L.E.K. Consulting Profiles the New Face of Blockbuster Drugs," *Marketwired*, July 13, 2011.

21. Pharmaceutical Technology Editors, *"Decades of Change for the Top Pharmaceutical Companies. Tracking Change from Spinoffs of Chemical Companies to Life-sciences Powerhouses,"* Jul 11, 2012, PTSM: Pharmaceutical Technology Sourcing and Management, Volume 8, Issue 7.

22. L.E.K. Consulting, "L.E.K. Consulting Profiles the New Face of Blockbuster Drugs," *Marketwired*, July 13, 2011.

23. CBISIGHTS, *"The United States of Unicorns: Every US Company Worth $1B+ in One Map,"* July 25, 2017, accessed January 19, 2018, https://www.cbinsights.com/research/startup-unicorns-us-map/?utm_source=hs_automation&utm_medium=email&utm_content=56699783&_hsenc=p2ANqtz-9UwKjh1kHVXiYqtwlNjZqWeEQoxHo-02QNHHZr4VfuMmbmdHrbefGGybdinJDBtOgTM2mThK-D9ZFaz6Q5la32_mpxoKBkfkOyRsxVl3NK3w9Jzxk&_hsmi=56699783

Chapter 2

The Unicorn Industry Loses Its Wings

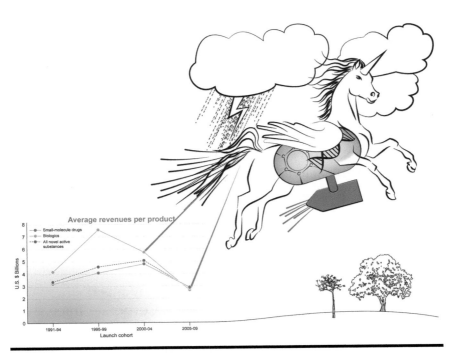

Unicorn industry loses speed and altitude.

"Rowing harder doesn't help if the boat is headed in the wrong direction."

Kenichi Ohmae

These days, stories of free gourmet food at tech giants are legendary. It is considered a key motivator for employees. In fact, an absence of free food in the tech industry may indicate that the company does not have the right culture in looking after employees. Let us call it the "Free Food Meter" to measure the health of industries. While the tech industry is the clear winner these days, in the late 1990s and early 2000s, gourmet, free or subsidized food in biopharma cafeterias was also the norm. Today, food subsidies are gone. Free coffee is becoming rare. And the "Free Food Meter" is indicating a decline in the industry's glory days.

With success comes the pressure to maintain progress. Right on the heels of a wildly successful period in the 1990s, marketing practices such as fully paid trips for physicians to exotic locations came into vogue and were often associated with increases in prescription volumes. While the FDA ensured that the scientific facts to prove safety and efficacy were valid, it was now the "wild west" of marketing and sales all over again. Consequently, the regulatory and compliance burdens increased as companies started to find themselves under government scrutiny for questionable marketing and sales activities. Sadly, this was not isolated— almost every major pharmaceutical company has been fined and found itself operating under a Corporate Integrity Agreement (CIA).

As the burden of healthcare costs is now becoming unsustainable for employers and government alike, the squeeze on the pricing of healthcare services and shifting of cost to consumers has become more real than ever.

Held hostage to margin expectations and declining true innovation that could drive premium pricing, the biopharma industry is experiencing the limits of its unicorn business model. In parallel with pricing pressure, the implementation and monitoring of CIAs are burdening companies with an increased level of generalized internal scrutiny, often in areas well beyond what triggered the initial inquiry, and an increase in operating procedures that tend to narrow the industry's role in the healthcare ecosystem to a supplier of biopharmaceutical products. As a result, the industry is facing an even more significant challenge to innovate outside the core of its historical biopharmaceutical product development and associated business model.

Regrettably, the case can also be made that continued focus on strengthening the proven commercial model and reliance on legal barriers creating market exclusivity has come at the expense of declining scientific innovation productivity. IDEA Pharma publishes an annual Productive Innovation Index (PII) which looks at FDA approvals. In 2016 approvals fell from 45 in 2015 to 22 in 2016. According to information released by the FDA, 2017 appears to have recorded an increase in new drug approvals closer to that of 2015. However, what may be more interesting than merely looking at total numbers is the observation that while 7 of the top 13 biopharmaceutical companies received 14 approvals in 2015, that same group delivered none in 2016. This finding suggests that despite its R&D investments approaching 20% of net sales, incumbents may no longer be nimble enough to provide a pipeline of new products necessary to support continued growth at a level sufficient to meet shareholder expectations.

There is also an on-going debate, usually in the context of pharmaceutical prices, about whether it is the private biopharmaceutical industry or the federal and state governments a.k.a. the taxpaying public that fund innovation through basic research carried out at NIH and public universities. Statements appear in the lay press claiming that up to 75% of New Molecular Entities (NMEs) receiving priority rating by the FDA can trace their funding back to the NIH. Biopharmaceutical manufacturers and their trade associations (Pharmaceutical Research and Manufacturers of America [PhRMA], Biotechnology Innovation Organization [BIO], National Pharmaceutical Council [NPC]) consistently point out that they lead most industrial sectors in R&D investment, both absolute and as a percent of net sales. Furthermore, they argue that it is not the cost of discovery that consumes the most resources. Instead, it is the process of developing and testing the biopharmaceutical product through the multi-year, highly regulated review process that drives total costs and commitment of resources, which must, therefore, be recouped through market exclusivity and free market pricing.

While both of these positions can be documented and defended, they miss the point we are trying to make, i.e., the debate continues to stay narrowly focused on pure biopharmaceutical product-based innovation overly reliant on the artificial market advantage created by regulation and still relatively healthy reimbursement rates in the United States. As the cost burden of healthcare increases to unsustainable levels and debate on the pricing of pharmaceuticals intensifies (accelerated by the enactment of the Affordable Care Act under President Obama), it is only a matter of time before the traditional high-margin business model enabled by regulation will begin to unravel. The ongoing consolidation in provider markets, where physicians are typically affiliated with and more recently employed by large provider networks, along with increased scrutiny designed to identify questionable marketing practices—including the Physician Payments Sunshine Act (PPSA) that is geared to drive transparency in biopharmaceutical industry payments to physicians—is placing further constraints on the ability of the industry's business model to generate revenue at historical levels. The overarching negative result is that precisely at the time leadership should be focused on finding new sources of innovation by challenging the status quo, they have mostly doubled down on protecting the core business, establishing consistency, minimizing variability, and maximizing profits.

The investor community mostly still believes in the pharmaceutical industry as one that can provide healthy returns. In our view, this is short-term thinking. We have discussed the fall-off in industry productivity as measured by new drug approvals and significant negative impact on pricing and therefore sales development resulting primarily from Pharmacy Benefit Managers (PBM) pressure which may be intensified by future government intervention. According to the 2017 Deloitte Center for Health Solutions report on "Measuring the Return from Pharmaceutical Innovation" in which they have followed the performance of 12 large cap biopharma companies for several years, they have observed that:

■ Peak sales/assets declined from $816 million in 2010 to $394 million in 2016 with a slight rebound in 2017 to $465 million;
■ Costs to bring an asset to market increased from $1.19 billion in 2010 to $1.99 billion in 2017; and
■ Return on R&D declined from 10.1% in 2009 to 3.2% in 2017.

Clearly, the biopharmaceutical industry is challenged in continuing to deliver its historical financial performance. If we consider the longer term—the next 20+ years—in our opinion, the following factors will further accelerate the disruption of the industry as we know it today:

■ Limited white spaces for traditional product-focused innovation
■ Therapies versus cures
■ Transition from old to new technology
■ Outcome and value versus safety and efficacy
■ Commoditization

- Consumerism
- New Disruptors
- Evolution of the regulatory framework as a source of disruption

Let us examine each in detail.

Limited White Spaces for Traditional Product-Focused Innovation

From a product innovation perspective, the industry has moved from tackling chronic diseases to specialty diseases to, more recently, rare diseases. It has looked at advances in genetics and genomics to become highly targeted in treatment efficacy. However, the disease states where a therapeutic product can provide competitive differentiation are getting more and more limited. There are over 7,000 known diseases, with only 500[1] with treatments or cures, and therefore the case could be made that there is plenty of room for continued product-based innovation. However, look a little closer, and it is obvious that we are getting into the realm of very rare diseases, where due to the small population size it is very difficult to find patients to conduct trials and treatments. Furthermore, the expectation on margins leads to very high drug prices facing both affordability challenges (third-party payers and patients) plus a growing demand to demonstrate cost-effectiveness at a time when people are beginning to find the concept of societal rationing more acceptable even in the United States. These factors provide evidence that the current model will fail at some point. In fact, we would argue that the biopharmaceutical industry has no more than 30 years left of the traditional business model—ten more years for exhausting remaining white spaces that can be addressed purely with molecule-based products, and another 20 years of patent life protection. We are potentially being liberal here with the timeframe should new environmental challenges appear. Within this time, commoditization of the business model we know today will accelerate.

Therapies versus Cures

One limitation of biopharmaceuticals has been that they are primarily therapeutic, not curative. As the cost of pharmaceuticals continues to be a significant area of public scrutiny, alternative therapies are establishing a strong foothold. In China and India—the largest consumer markets—traditional Chinese medicine, Ayurveda, healthy lifestyles, and healthy nutrition focused on prevention are in vogue. Local governments are investing in developing evidence for the effectiveness of these therapies similar to the approach adopted by western biopharmaceutical industry, and also in training programs to develop licensed practitioners of traditional medicine. In the western world, there is an entire movement focused on wellness and prevention—looking to solve for healthcare costs by reducing demand for healthcare and adopting healthy living and eating practices from the eastern world, including meditation and yoga. Digital health-based therapeutics are emerging as equally effective yet lower-cost alternatives to biopharmaceuticals. For example, Omada Health's Prevent has been found effective in managing pre-diabetes. Twine is focused on the management of hypertension.[2]

"The term 'digital therapeutics' refers to using a digital system to treat a medical condition, much as one might use a drug, a human counselor, or surgery. Digital therapeutics are used both stand-alone and in combination with conventional therapies."[3] We propose a broader concept of Smart integrated Medicine or S[i]M later in the book.

Further, the role of vaccines can't be overlooked. In fact, most global epidemics have been managed through vaccination—be it diphtheria, cholera, yellow fever, or polio. At the simplest level, vaccines work by strengthening our natural biological system to fight against these diseases. It does so by training our body to generate disease-fighting T cells and B cells when pathogens triggering these disorders are detected in the body. A very diluted or killed version of the pathogen is typically injected into the body to train these T cells and B cells to fight any actual future infection. Today, companies like Modern Therapeutics and Gritstone Oncology are looking at developing cancer vaccines that could disrupt the current business model for oncology treatments. There are ongoing advances in the field of regenerative medicine where organs grown in natural (e.g., animals such as pigs and sheep) or engineered growth systems could replace diseased organs in the human body, limiting the need for therapeutic medication.

Outcome and Value versus Safety and Efficacy

There is a new sheriff in town. Sole reliance on safety and efficacy claims doesn't cut it anymore. As societies get smarter over time, they expect more from everything, including products generated by the biopharmaceutical industry. In the new world, safety and efficacy are table stakes. What is needed is proof that the product is effective at the individual patient level and that there is a stronger relationship between the product and the outcome of using the product. Proving effectiveness in large populations which forms the cornerstone of the modern drug development paradigm has inherent limitations. By definition, one can only detect average responses to medication in RCTs or retrospective population-level data analytics of insurance claims or treatment history. As a result, patients outside of the "average outcome" range are not necessarily receiving the best therapeutic option or an optimal dose at any time. The current focus of population health management initiatives on measuring average responses at the population level, while well-intentioned, may turn out to be a fad or at best insufficient. Ultimately, it is the individual patient/consumer experience that will determine effectiveness (clinical and cost) of the outcome and therefore reimbursement.

Should the industry adopt new reimbursement models, for example, the individual pays only for the outcome they experience? Will the mainstream industry sit by while outsiders solve the problem of how to measure and be compensated for individualized treatments and outcomes? There is an increasing number of experiments in value- or outcomes-based contracting being publicized by both manufacturers and payers, but these are only small first steps toward universally available value-based care.

Transition from Old to New Technology

In any other industry, the lack of underlying technology innovation would have been the reason for a company's quick demise. Imagine today's technology industry if it still depended on the first two programming languages that were the basis of its foundation—BASIC and COBOL. Further, the lack of commercial model innovation typically leads to declining competitive advantage and the rise of new entrants. However, the biopharmaceutical industry has managed not only to survive, but also remain highly profitable over the past 30+ years after harnessing the power of synthetic chemistry and biotechnology despite a lack of subsequent underlying technology or commercial model innovation. Gene therapy, Clustered Regularly Interspaced Short Palindromic Repeats (CRISPR), and Chimeric Antigen Receptor (CAR)-T can be viewed as three new "programming languages" for the industry that may signal the next wave of core innovation. CRISPR enables selective gene editing to cure genetic diseases.

The first FDA approved example of direct gene therapy is based on utilizing a modified viral vector to deliver a new, functional gene into a cell. This technology that is the underlying basis of other upcoming treatments. CAR-T focuses on conveying patient-specific T cell targeting capabilities against certain types of cancer. All three technologies offer considerable promise and hold the potential for driving a new wave of innovative biopharmaceutical products, but the majority of industry investment and revenue generation remains linked to the traditional product-based model. Specific examples of applying these new technology platforms are available. Kymriah (Novartis) is the first CAR-T cell therapy approved by the FDA for treatment of acute lymphoblastic leukemia in children and young adults. Needing only one administration, Kymriah has been shown to be effective in 80% of patients. Similarly, Luxturna (Spark Therapeutics), also approved in 2017, is the first of its kind gene therapy that with one administration can treat a rare type of inherited vision loss. While these are great examples of innovation, the high price—$475,000 in the case of Kymriah and $425,000 per eye for Luxturna—have heightened the debate across the healthcare ecosystem on the value and reimbursement for these treatments. According to Joseph La Barge, Chief Legal Officer at Spark, the feedback from the payer community has to date been cautiously positive because of innovative steps Spark has taken to incentivize availability and access. Some of the key elements of its strategy include a new distribution model that shields hospitals/health systems from upfront product acquisition costs and agreements with payers that may involve a refund if patients don't maintain improvements to functional vision over a pre-defined period of time. Spark is also in negotiations with the Centers for Medicare and Medicaid Services, the federal government health insurance agency, to come up with ways to let insurers pay by installments and enable greater rebates tied to clinical outcomes as part of pay-for-performance agreements that don't trigger the negative impact of Medicaid best-price implications which, as we discuss later in this chapter, can inhibit innovation in pricing models. Taken together these can be viewed as a big first step along the journey of moving from paying for product to paying for outcomes. Along with the pricing and reimbursement innovation, Spark's customer-engagement model is more dependent on medical to medical communication and providing superior customer service than the conventional biopharmaceutical rep to physician sales force model.

While these new technologies could lead to a shift in the industry from being primarily therapeutic-focused toward a curative model, the development of innovation in those spaces has been slow. We hope that the technology advances briefly noted here can serve as a catalyst for innovation in the incumbents' commercial model. Future cures will also require more radical models in financing and insurance, especially given the current U.S. fragmentation of payment as people change the source of coverage throughout their lives. For example, there is an on-going debate as to who or which entity should pay to cure a disease that typically manifests in advanced age, an employer upon initial identification of the opportunity or the Center for Medicare and Medicaid Services (CMS) to avoid future costs when the patient would be Medicare eligible?

Commoditization

In most societies, at least in the developed world, healthcare is considered a right, not a privilege. Governments can gain a lot of political capital by ensuring that the cost of healthcare remains low. The cost of pharmaceuticals can be readily isolated and managed relative to other elements of the complex and fragmented healthcare value chain, and all governments do it using a variety of approaches. Given that

10.7% of the world population lives on less than \$1.90/day (extreme poverty)[4] and the next ~50% on less than \$10 per day (low income),[5] the markets where companies can afford to charge high prices are limited. The U.S. market (where companies have the most pricing power and have historically used it to compensate for lower price markets) is facing a significant financial crisis as the cost of healthcare continues to rise approaching 20% of the GDP. That level of GDP investment in healthcare is unsustainable and will continue to disrupt the pricing power of the industry and associated margins. As a result, we will see pricing parity across the globe over time, challenging industry profitability highly dependent on U.S. markets.

Companies that have transitioned their portfolio from small molecule-based products for chronic diseases that are readily commoditized by Pharmacy Benefit Managers to specialty products for smaller populations have gained some short-term buffer to net pricing pressure and may, therefore, be lulled into a sense that the current core business is enough. However, it is already evident that even highly innovative products (by traditional standards) launched at premiums for existing therapies can be readily commoditized when there is more than one alternative. A recent case study can be seen in the newer hepatitis C products. Although they cured a previously difficult-to-manage disease in most patients and could avoid financial and societal costs associated with liver transplants, they came under severe public scrutiny and pricing pressure due to affordability challenges, and the benefits were largely overlooked. Despite all of the noise about using the benefits of treatments used to justify high prices at the time of introduction, U.S. net prices are now estimated to be lower than in most of Europe within two years after launch. Such a rapid erosion in net price illustrates the power that Pharmacy Benefit Managers have within the current free market when even highly innovative products can be viewed as interchangeable. Moreover, cost trumps the freedom of prescribing choice and the merits of individualized treatment.

On-going discussions about indication-based pricing, incentives/penalties for providers linked to following treatment guidelines, and payment tied to clinical outcome demonstrate that pricing even for oncology products previously regarded as off-limits by payers will face similar pressure soon. The problem is further compounded by the fact that the payment systems are fragmented and not transparent except for patient co-pays which are influenced not so much by the merits of individual products but by the willingness of a single manufacturer to pay rebates during the contracting process.

Ongoing consolidation in the industry is a clear indicator that the industry is feeling the pressure of commoditization. It is looking to leverage scale as an opportunity to protect its pricing power, and maintain margins to allow continued investment in future R&D.

"PricewaterhouseCoopers and Bloomberg both predicted the drug cost to the healthcare system for AbbVie's Viekira Pak, for hepatitis C, and BMS' Opdivo, for metastatic melanoma skin cancer. Their predictions for Viekira Pak were over $2.9 billion; actual first-year sales were 28% of the prediction. The predicted cost of Opdivo was $1.7 billion; actual sales were 48% of predicted." Historically, "underestimates were less common—Novartis' Cosentyx, initially approved for psoriasis, was predicted to cost $120 million in the first year after launch; actual sales were more than twice that. (The Partnership for Health Analytics Research [PHAR]) looked at predictions for 14 drugs launched since 2012: the PCSK9s, three oncology drugs, three for hepatitis C, two for obesity management, and one each for cystic fibrosis, heart failure, psoriasis, and diabetes. On average, pre-launch predictions were 11 times higher than actual sales."[6]

Consumerism

In the United States, either the national health system or employer-sponsored health insurance has paid for healthcare. However, as the burden of healthcare as a percentage of GDP continues to rise, two things are happening. One, the payers of healthcare are looking for cost efficiencies wherever they can find them, and two, they are shifting the cost burden to the individual wherever possible. In India, where healthcare is primarily a self-care market, healthcare is a privilege. If you have money, you get care; if you don't have money, you get aspirin. In such an environment, people shop for best prices and consume less. As the cost burden in the western world continues to shift toward the consumer, similar to the developing world, healthcare will become a privilege, not a right. This, in turn, will reduce consumption (demand) and therefore either constrain supply or drive down prices. Alternatively, consumers will become much more informed and selective in purchasing decisions similar to the way in which they are buying other goods and services following principles of behavioral economics. Both result in a downward pressure on the industry. In the United States, where the healthcare industry consumes most money per capita (USD 8,745 versus OECD average of USD 3,454 versus India at USD 157),[7] we already see evidence of this trend in the form of High Deductible Health Plans, Consumer Driven Health Plans, and employer-sponsored private healthcare exchanges which often feature narrower benefits than those more traditional health plan benefit designs offered by self-insured employers. Ultimately, such developments will continue to drive pressures in the biopharmaceutical industry in its last remaining bastion of pricing power—the United States of America.

In the face of these trends, the traditional biopharmaceutical industry incumbents are doubling down on efforts to sustain the IP protection of products to be able to harvest the market opportunity for as long as possible, while trying to find efficiencies in all other aspects of the development and commercial enterprise. In one example of creativity, in 2017 Allergan decided to protect its patent for Restasis by selling the patent to a Native American tribe and securing an exclusive license back. Because the tribes have sovereignty over their jurisdictions, the patents presumably became more difficult to be challenged by the inter partes review (IPR) process, a process which has proven unpredictable in the past. As of February 2018, the Patent Trial and Appeal Board has struck down a motion by the tribe to dismiss the IPR for Restasis. While it will be interesting to watch as to how the story develops, this tactic has been perceived as an act of desperation on the part of the industry and generally a failure. It showcases an over-dependence on legal protections versus technological innovation in driving its profits.

Looking across industries, there are none that rely so heavily on market exclusivity as the rationale for innovation investments as does the biopharmaceutical sector. In fact, almost every other industry competes on customer value and experience and is embracing the changing consumption expectations driven by generational shifts. In the United States, it is estimated that by 2020 one in every three adults will be a millennial.[8] Ernst & Young estimates that by 2025 three quarters of the global workforce will consist of millennials.[9] They have grown up with technology and expect experiences that are shaped within their "always on" digital co-existence. Two industries that come to mind are financial services/insurance and automotive. For the former, as they evolve to embrace the challenge of digital transformation, one of the keys to success is the need to make customer experiences a pivotal part of the business model. In a crowded, price-competitive market, optimizing the experience that customers receive across devices and channels can bring fresh opportunities for business growth and higher market share, primarily by attracting millennials to replace the dominant boomer market segment. In today's automotive market, shoppers routinely use the Internet as the primary research tool to guide their purchase decisions, as well as a platform for sharing customer experience and feedback. In such an information-intensive environment both automakers and dealerships must employ data to better understand the needs, desires, and journeys of their customers as they make purchasing decisions. Such an upheaval is necessary across industries given that the next generation, Gen Z, is growing up to be digital innates: that is, technology is part of their cognitive conscience. Most young children around us today learn to play games on iPads and interact with technology before they learn to speak. As they grow up and drive consumption, products and services that don't meet their native digital existence will become relics of the past.

New Disruptors

There was a time when the biopharmaceutical industry was able to sustain a competitive advantage based on the high cost of entry associated with the investment required in bringing products to market and the virtual product monopolies it created through intellectual property protection and regulation. However, the industry is currently experiencing a new kind of competition. Everyone has their eye on the $3 trillion healthcare market, projected to grow to $18 trillion by 2040, or 9% of the world's GDP.[10] Companies like Apple and Google have large piles of cash (more than the biopharmaceutical industry) that they are looking to invest. They own the relationships with the end users of healthcare, the patients (consumers). They see a prime opportunity to make money in the healthcare market and are making multiple investments to gain their share of this immense pie. They are hiring experts from academia and the mainstream industry and encouraging them to develop platform technologies in an unstructured fashion without regard to a pre-defined disease state or target patient population which in many ways is in direct opposition to the approach taken by the incumbents. Furthermore, they don't have to worry about legacy costs that are entrenched within the biopharmaceutical industry. As a result, they can disrupt the biopharmaceutical industry not only through products they bring to market, but also on the development and commercialization cost model. While these are still early days of their foray into the healthcare space, the biopharmaceutical industry is at the same time threatened and lulled into comfort given its business model. However, in the future, in the absence of a significant pivot by the biopharmaceutical industry, the tech industry could be the dominant player in healthcare.

We tested the level of threat from outsiders with a few of our industry colleagues, and there is a range of views. Don Sawyer, Senior Vice President, Market Access and GM of Established Products for Bayer's U.S. organization does not see a tech outsider such as Verily or Amazon completely disrupting and displacing the biopharmaceutical industry. Although he does believe that some biopharmaceutical companies will eventually invest enough of their R&D budget through partnerships with new entrants to move beyond a core product-focused business model and gain a significant competitive advantage. Blasine Penkowski, Chief Strategic Customer Officer at the Janssen Division of J&J, believes that there is a fundamental problem with the patient experience within the current healthcare system resulting from fragmentation of patient touch points. In her view, solving for a seamless customer experience is an opportunity for integrators that could come from multiple sectors. She can see the potential impact of an organization like Amazon on distribution and groups such as Teladoc displacing some elements of the current relationship between providers and patients. She does not see this as a negative if, for example, displacing more common diagnoses and treatment to technology can free up providers to focus on more complex health problems.

We have to wait and see the dynamic tension between how fast incumbents can change, the degree to which the industry will be disrupted from outside, and who from among the new entrants will be the winners. We will not have to wait long though.

Evolution of the Regulatory Framework as a Source of Disruption

The modern biopharmaceutical industry has mastered the product development process within a regulatory framework that is designed to ensure new products enter the market with a high level of scrutiny and demonstration of an acceptable risk-benefit profile. Other regulations place boundaries on the type and timing of conversations that can occur between the industry and its customers and stakeholders. Those regulations have also in some ways served as a barrier to entrants from outside the mainstream industry. Given the overriding mandate of the FDA to protect the safety of the U.S. population, it also has mostly been a conservative organization, slow to embrace change. Increasing impatience by the public regarding access to new medical innovation coupled with the rapid emergence of new technology is challenging the FDA to move faster. Also, outrage across multiple sectors over pharmaceutical prices and certain commercial activities that may be viewed by some as anti-competitive (e.g., so-called "pay-to-delay" agreements between originator and generic companies) have triggered a potential willingness to broaden the FDA's and other agencies's historical sphere of influence. This is true even in a political environment dominated by the Republican party which traditionally resists government expansion. These changes can be viewed as either positive or negative by incumbents depending on the way they have defined their innovation agenda as either being grounded in their historical core or open to new opportunities. A number of these potential changes are described below.

A Pathway toward Accelerated Approval of Digital Health

In 2017, the FDA announced a pre-certification pilot program ultimately intended to streamline the review/approval process for digital health products and solutions by looking at the competencies and track record of the software or digital health technology developer, rather than at the product itself. They selected nine organizations across the medical device and technology sectors to participate in the pilot program, five of which are technology companies (Apple, Fitbit, Samsung, Tidepool, and Verily). Only two biopharmaceutical incumbents (Johnson & Johnson and Roche) made the list. Phosphorus (diagnostics) and Pear Therapeutics (digital therapeutics) complete the roster. Commissioner Scott Gottlieb M.D. framed these potential regulatory changes in the context of the iterative characteristics of digital health products, and therefore the need for a regulatory framework that is aligned with the kind of innovation the FDA is being asked to evaluate. This demonstration of attitudes and principles consistent with application of the 80-80 Rule should be an eye-opener for the biopharmaceutical industry.

Accelerated Approval of Generics and Linkage to Price Concerns

As noted earlier, the Hatch–Waxman amendment created clarity around the regulatory abbreviated new drug application (ANDA) approval process for small molecule generics. This legislation has been mostly successful in rapidly (sometimes virtually overnight) bringing down prices once two or more generics are approved which has then freed up funding to pay for innovation. However, there are multiple products for which the compound patent has long expired and yet for a variety of reasons there are no generics available. This supports higher prices sometimes at a level that has triggered public and government outrage. In response, the FDA has increased the priority of generic approvals by focusing on those ANDA eligible products with no or limited generic availability. While the FDA has historically avoided the topic of drug costs and pricing, the new commissioner has characterized access to affordable medications as a public health issue thus potentially signaling changes in attitude on this subject, further challenging the pricing power of the biopharmaceutical industry.

Attitudes toward Real World Evidence

The cornerstone of the product development and regulatory review process has been the elaborate and expensive RCT which does a great job in isolating the effect of the new product to reduce confounding factors and variation due to chance. However, it also means that new products sometimes do not perform the same way in the real world setting regarding safety and efficacy as they do during the development process. The 21st Century Cures Act of 2016 contains provisions related to the use of Real World Evidence (RWE) defining it somewhat loosely as "data regarding the usage, or the potential benefits or risks, of a drug derived from sources other than randomized clinical trials." The act requires the Secretary of the Department of Health and Human Services to develop a program for evaluating the use of RWE with the goal that such alternative data sources will increasingly be used to support new indications for drugs already on the market and to fulfill post-marketing study requirements. Should this initial experiment prove fruitful, it could open the way for broader use of RWE in the new product approval process and thereby lower the investment and relatively closed system that the biopharma industry has dominated to date, potentially creating opportunities for non-traditional solution providers to enter the market. FDA Commissioner Gottlieb has added his personal commitment to encourage use of RWE across multiple areas over which the FDA has jurisdiction, re-enforcing the potential impact of shifting attitudes toward Real World Evidence.

Deliberations Focused on Removing Barriers that Have Inhibited Value-Based Care

There have been several recent discussions regarding legal and regulatory barriers that may hinder the adoption of value-based healthcare. Two examples are the Medicaid best-price and the Stark Law governing relationships between hospitals and physicians. Medicaid law requires that its beneficiaries always receive the best or lowest price for biopharmaceutical products relative to all purchasing entities (for example, Medicare, Commercial Insurers, and even Veterans Affairs and Department of Defense). This requirement could result in adverse revenue implications for a biopharmaceutical company that was willing to offer prices linked to clinical outcomes. For example, consider a situation in which a product is initially launched at a price linked to a highly effective result in indication A. If the manufacturer was subsequently willing to offer a lower, value-based price for indication B where the product has less impressive efficacy, the best-price condition could result in having to lower the price for Medicaid patients treated even for indication A in which efficacy was stronger. Clearly, this would penalize a manufacturer even though it was willing to offer differentiated pricing based on relative efficacy. Regarding the Stark law, the American Hospital Association and others have requested that Congress adopt a single but broad exception to federal fraud and abuse laws related to financial relationships between parties that could break down silos and foster the type of collaboration needed to deliver improvements in healthcare via new payment models. These are just a number of emerging trends that could benefit both incumbents (if they are willing to challenge their historical ways of working) and outsiders who don't need to overcome the status quo but would rather embrace the new approaches as they enter the healthcare sector.

Communication with Payers and Providers during the Pre-Commercialization Period

Often concerns about pricing of new biopharmaceutical products arise from an affordability perspective and especially when there may not have been a budget provision to pay for the upcoming innovation. Payers would undoubtedly like to have access to information earlier in the pre-approval timeframe to adequately budget, and biopharmaceutical manufacturers would find it useful to engage in such discussions to ascertain coverage. However, concerns about compliance with pre-promotion limitations and significant uncertainty over the interpretation of the Food and Drug Administration Modernization Act of 1997, section 14 (FDAMA 114), have significantly curtailed such discussions. Proposed changes contained in the 21st Century Cures Act add some clarity and flexibility for pharmaceutical companies to engage with health insurance companies about the potential value of their products. The legislation defines and broadens the type of information that can be shared by biopharmaceutical manufacturers and who can receive such relevant information, for example, explicitly adding payers to the list. While there is considerable work needed to clarify how to implement these intentions it is a positive step in enhancing the necessary dialogue thereby accelerating reimbursement for new products.

To someone from outside the industry, these changes may seem minor and imminently logical. The critical question is whether incumbents will recognize and seize the opportunity to make these changes to accelerate their innovation agenda transformation. To some degree, biopharma insiders remain focused on the argument that they are often unfairly singled out as the source of healthcare cost drivers because direct patient impact in the form of pharmacy benefit premiums and co-pays are evident at the point of sale. On the other hand, other components such as out-patient medical care, diagnostic procedures, and hospitalization costs are masked by a complex interplay of list prices that no one pays, negotiated insurance payments, and write-offs. The incumbent industry can attempt to continue to deflect the increasing legislative pressures through some mix of moderating list price increases, clarifying the relative contribution of biopharmaceuticals to total costs and calling attention to the role of other healthcare industry stakeholders in driving healthcare costs. In our view, they might be better served by embracing the changes outlined previously. If implemented, these changes would signal a significant disruption in what has been a series of hurdles and barriers for outsiders to challenge the business model practiced by biopharmaceutical incumbents and potentially open the market to new players. In such a scenario, proactive self-disruption through redefining innovation might be the only smart choice for the industry.

An Industry Perspective

To test our challenging hypotheses on the future of the biopharmaceutical industry, we have spoken with several stakeholders across the healthcare ecosystem. Given the rapid pace of change and a wide range of experiences faced by individual organizations, it should be no surprise that there is a commensurate range of views on the long-term viability of a biopharma innovation model grounded in the current new product discovery and development paradigm and reactions to some of our key points. Some of these differences in response can be attributed to a particular company's product portfolio and research pipeline. Some biopharmaceutical incumbents continue to focus mainly on products for more common, chronic diseases impacting a significant number of patients while others have shifted their focus to what the FDA designates as breakthrough therapies based on new technologies that we have highlighted earlier for diseases impacting increasingly rare populations.

Paul Fonteyne, CEO of Boehringer Ingelheim in the United States, noted that the biopharmaceutical industry might view some of these changes, resulting pressures, and predictions regarding the demise of the biopharma industry as a "movie we have seen before." He believes there is still significant opportunity for biopharmaceutical companies to innovate within their historical core while recognizing that the threshold for success continues to rise. He acknowledges that companies that have elected to stay focused on sizable chronic disease states will investigate adjacencies in digital health, new payment models, etc., that could lead to new business opportunities in the future.

Don Sawyer, Senior Vice President, Bayer is well aligned to the need for the biopharma industry to broaden its definition of innovation. He believes the industry has been a victim of its success with the blockbuster model of the past. It masked a "multitude of sins" in terms of inefficiencies. When things got tough, the typical industry response was to acquire with the goal of buying growth. In his view, the unwillingness of biopharma incumbents to experiment outside the traditional product discovery/commercialization model is because such efforts have unproven results, coupled with a focus on delivering near term Return on Investment (ROI) expectations. While the industry has become better at understanding failure in traditional R&D, no similar risk-taking attitude exists in most commercial organizations. He spoke about his experience at a prior company where R&D "failures" were celebrated based on terminating projects early to avoid wasting resources. He contrasted this with the observation that the only time a person in most commercial organizations is celebrated for taking risks and failing is at their going away party.

Blasine Penkowski, Chief Strategic Customer Officer from the Janssen division of J&J says that payers/PBMs have increasingly implemented tactics such as exclusion lists for a larger number of therapeutic categories and therefore success in the biopharmaceutical industry depends more than ever on meaningful innovation to address significant unmet medical needs. She notes that it is important for the entire biopharmaceutical industry, including researchers, to understand the payer perspective and focus on innovation that will be valued in the marketplace because of the real difference it makes for patients. When asked why J&J seems to be ahead of other biopharma incumbents in establishing new ventures such as J-Labs, she suggested that since the company occupies multiple healthcare sectors including OTC products and Medical Devices, they may have understood pressures in the healthcare system earlier than pure-play pharmaceutical companies.

In summary, most biopharma executives and observers we spoke with agree with the premise that the industry faces challenges at a level not seen historically, and that the industry is beginning to broaden its views on the need to innovate the commercial model, particularly in the way it demonstrates the value proposition of new products in the context of total healthcare costs versus focusing only on the biopharmaceutical component. They uniformly highlight the need for a new legal and regulatory framework to support the industry's innovative payment models as we have described earlier and expect to see more innovative approaches regarding healthcare financing including biopharmaceuticals in the future. Some executives with whom we spoke envision new opportunities for supporting patients with wrap-around services that can complement new therapies and support the view that these may be best delivered through new types of collaborations and partnerships across manufacturers, technology providers, payers, and providers. As noted, there is a range of views on the future of the current biopharmaceutical business model with some executives remaining bullish as long as the industry continues to develop new products that address real unmet needs and employ breakthrough technology.

The Future?

Only time will tell if the current challenges to the biopharmaceutical industry will turn out to be just another storm that will pass as long as industry incumbents continue to drive core business by bringing innovative new molecules to market, co-exist with other industry incumbents, and protect their position on Capitol Hill. However, as the industry looks inward, it should realize that it is rapidly losing many of the levers beyond the now threatened commercial model, and the barriers to entry for outsiders, that have historically been significant sources of competitive advantage:

a. The scientific talent within the industry is graying, and new talent is not making the mainstream biopharma industry its first choice. Much of the best talent in medicine and life sciences is now going to the tech industry and startups that are increasingly blurring traditional distinction between sectors.

b. The reliance on research process discipline practiced repetitively and driven by Standard Operating Procedures and proprietary methods as a differentiator is ready to be disrupted by new technology such as

Artificial Intelligence and Machine Learning. These technologies can be rapidly adopted and applied by new entrants from outside the industry who have access to consumer health, claims or medical records data that can drive future research.

c. The FDA and other regulatory bodies are simplifying their processes to encourage innovation and completion. At the same time, the industry has been outsourcing the process for long enough that the expertise is now readily available on the open market and no longer a source of competitive advantage.

d. One could argue that the biopharmaceutical industry has always been a data analytics and insights industry. It has generated and communicated data that has been the value proposition in the market versus the physical product. However, we could also argue the data analytics in the industry has always been very controlled, shared only to the extent necessitated by regulations, and rarely an explicit representation of product performance in the real market. In today's culture obsessed with value and transparency, the industry has to get ready for deep data analytics capabilities to be able to provide real-world data on the performance of their products. However, as mentioned, much of the talent sits outside of the industry.

In most industries, the boom-to-bust cycles for companies are very short. It is estimated that "in 1965, the average tenure of companies on the S&P 500 was 33 years. By 1990, it was 20 years, and it's forecast to shrink to 14 years by 2026."[11] The biopharmaceutical industry has been fortunate that longevity of the biggest companies in its sector driven by mergers and acquisitions has allowed it to remain relevant for a much longer time. Some companies have become akin to mutual fund companies—it is really about portfolio management. We will continue to see further consolidation. Interestingly, the industry has enjoyed the unicorn status only in the last 20 years, and therefore its ongoing disruption may be aligned to the typical industry lifecycles. Very soon, we will most likely be left with a small number of large portfolio management companies. They will be supported and enabled by multiple early-stage start-ups that function entirely as lead generators building their model on up-front payments and royalties and avoiding commercialization start-up and infrastructure costs, or eventually get consumed by these portfolio managers.

At a minimum, the biopharmaceutical industry needs to consider how to foster and embrace these changes that will otherwise challenge its historical dominance. Incumbents need to pause and consider what will sustain them for the long term. We are talking here about companies that will exist for the next 100 years, not the next ten years. Most people would agree that 20 years from now, the industry will look very different from what it has been for the last 100 years, given the rapidly narrowing space for product-focused innovation, technological advances, and economic pressures. We can already see some evidence of the willingness of the mainstream industry to innovate in the core which could spawn adjacencies. Dan Leonard, President of National Pharmaceutical Council (NPC), the industry association focused on Evidence-Based Medicine and Value, confirmed that member companies are primarily focused on innovation related to biopharmaceutical products. However, he views the work that is being sponsored on researching alternative and outcomes-based payment models, incorporating Real World Evidence in the development and commercialization process, and positioning pharmaceuticals in the broader context of the healthcare value chain, as evidence that the industry is committed to innovating within the core to a greater magnitude than what was seen historically.

We are reasonably confident that the industry of the future will not be dominated by companies that elect to continue focusing only on new chemical and biological entities, developed for increasingly rare diseases with smaller patient populations that must, therefore, command higher prices to be economically viable. Coming back to the earlier movie reference, given all of the factors that we have cited that represent challenges and disrupters, while the traditional biopharma innovation model may be analogous to a movie script that has spun several successful sequels, it may have now run its course. This doesn't necessarily mean that the studio needs to close because in the next section on redefining innovation we offer an alternative view of how the industry can leverage the competencies that made it successful in the past to refresh its storyline.

The critical question is whether the sector will be dominated by today's incumbents that have successfully adopted principles consistent with the 80–80 Rule and transformed their innovation engine and business model or will be governed by new players from outside the current sector not "burdened" by past success. We are confident that at least some of today's successful companies will determine how to leverage their core capabilities, relatively high margins, and the barriers to outsiders to evolve their innovation agenda and business model in time. Part of that optimism is grounded in our own experiences that gave rise to the idea for this book.

Endnotes

1. Fred Upton and Diana DeGette, *"Can We Find Cures for 7,000 Diseases?"* *CNN.com*, January 13, 2015, accessed January 19, 2018, http://www.cnn.com/2015/01/13/opinion/upton-degette-cure-diseases/index.html
2. Todd Hixon, *"Digital Therapeutics Have Huge Promise and They Are Real Today,"* *Fortune.com*, December 9, 2015, accessed January 19, 2018, https://www.forbes.com/sites/toddhixon/2015/12/09/digital-therapeutics-have-huge-promise-and-they-are-real-today/#6241851426f0

3. Joseph C. Kvedar, *The Internet of Healthy Things*, (The Internet of Healthy Things, 2015).

4. The World Bank, *"Understanding Poverty,"* accessed January 19, 2018, http://www.worldbank.org/en/topic/poverty/overview

5. Rakesh Kochhar, *"A Global Middle Class Is More Promise than Reality,"* Pew Research Center, August 13, 2015, accessed January 19, 2018, http://www.pewglobal.org/2015/07/08/a-global-middle-class-is-more-promise-than-reality/

6. "Where Are those Missing Billions in New-Product Pharma Sales?" *Pharmaceutical Commerce*, August 30, 2016, accessed January 19, 2018, http://pharmaceuticalcommerce.com/business-and-finance/missing-billions-new-product-pharma-sales/

7. OECD.gov, *"OECD Health Statistics 2014. How Does India Compare,"* accessed January 19, 2018, http://www.oecd.org/els/health-systems/Briefing-Note-INDIA-2014.pdf

8. Fred Dews, "11 Facts about the Millennial Generation," *Brookings Institute*, June 2, 2014.

9. Ernst & Young, *"Global Generations: A Global Study on Work-Life Challenges across Generations,"* 2015.

10. Institute for Health Metrics and Evaluation, *"Global Spending on Health Is Expected to Increase to $18.28 Trillion Worldwide by 2040 but Many Countries Will Miss Important Health Benchmarks,"* accessed January 19, 2018, http://www.healthdata.org/news-release/global-spending-health-expected-increase-1828-trillion-worldwide-2040-many-countries

11. Ilan Mochari, *"Why Half of the S&P 500 Companies Will Be Replaced in the Next Decade,"* Inc.com, accessed January 19, 2018, https://www.inc.com/ilan-mochari/innosight-sp-500-new-companies.html

Chapter 3

An Experiment in Challenging the Status Quo

"Any business today that embraces the status quo is going to be on a death march."

Howard Schultz

As we have noted, the pace of change in the healthcare environment and its impact on the biopharmaceutical industry has been intensifying and accelerating for some time. The Patient Protection and Affordable Care Act (PPACA) or Obamacare, enacted in March 2010 and effective January 2011, was just one more catalyst. As a positive, the industry eventually benefited from an increase in covered patient populations although mainly in the least profitable Medicaid segment impacted by best-price requirements. On the other hand, the immediate impact, i.e., new taxes on the industry and further responsibility to cover patients' Medicare Part D covered drug costs (self-administered prescription drugs, as opposed to Medicare Part B covered drugs that are administered by physicians in a clinical setting) while they experienced the "donut hole" coverage gap, was mostly viewed as detrimental to the industry. This regulation was such a dramatic event that virtually every biopharma company and many players across the healthcare ecosystem were forced to examine some of their business fundamentals.

U.S. healthcare industry post Obamacare.

Challenging the Status Quo

Our previous employer had enjoyed a long run of successful market performance with a portfolio of primary-care products, including favorable formulary positioning at what in retrospect was a moderate level of rebates. However, the business challenges that the biopharmaceutical industry's customers, typically payers and providers, were increasingly facing related to rising costs and market changes were amplified by the Affordable Care Act (ACA). It contributed to an environment in which relationships became more adversarial and transactional. Providers were consolidating and placing increased restrictions on pharmaceutical sales representatives' access thus challenging the fundamentals of the commercial model the industry had been reliant on for the last few decades. Payers and pharmacy benefit managers were moving toward closed formularies in which pharmaceutical products were no longer managed merely through co-pay tiers and preferred versus non-preferred classification but increasingly using exclusion lists narrowing the range of products available within a therapeutic category that were deemed clinically interchangeable through an opaque review process.

As the head of Managed Markets at Boehringer Ingelheim U.S. from 2009 to late 2015, I (Jeff) experienced first-hand the challenges related to massive uncertainty associated with the ACA and more demanding business conditions faced by our B2B customers during meetings that made negotiations for coverage of pharmaceutical products tougher than ever. However, now and then you could sense that this unprecedented level of uncertainty might create an opening for new types of conversations and a willingness by at least some customers to contemplate a new way of working. When individuals and organizations no longer believe they have all the answers they are sometimes more willing to step back and re-evaluate how they have traditionally viewed the way they work. This extremely challenging business environment coupled with observations regarding emerging customer behavior was the starting point for experiments to begin to define a new customer-facing model within the company.

A few like-minded individuals in the company engaged a consulting firm to assist in thinking through a new way of working with payers and organized providers. Our key hypotheses were that long-term formal partnerships, governed by multi-year contracts grounded in identifying fundamental challenges to healthcare funding and delivery and then harnessing the collective experience and resources of each party to address gaps, would begin to change customer relationships. The goal was to move engagements from transactions to partnerships that could jointly solve healthcare ecosystem problems. While there was a relatively wide range of responses from customers with which we explored interest in new ways to engage, we were ultimately successful in developing one Organized Customer Collaboration (OCC) with a nationally recognized payer organization.[1]

To enable and support planning and to carry out work through the OCC engagements, we established a small dedicated team. The dedicated team was to be supported by a flexible matrix team and a governance model comprised of individuals at different levels in the organization representing the entire product development and commercialization process. We hired a leader for this team (Ruchin) who set up the group, executed additional partnerships with payer and provider organizations and developed a robust portfolio of collaborative projects spanning clinical development, predictive modeling, pragmatic studies, clinical decision support systems, and provider and patient engagement.[2,3,4,5] He then went on to expand and broaden the remit of the team to develop capabilities in Digital Health. The team was responsible for the launch of a "first-of-its-kind commercial partnership with Propeller Health to use digital health tools and services to help people living with chronic obstructive pulmonary disease (COPD) and asthma better manage their disease."[6] Under Ruchin's leadership, the OCC and Digital Health efforts were then further extended toward the establishment of a Business Innovation function working on behalf of the entire organization.

While the deliberations and agreement negotiations associated with the early Organized Customer Collaborations seemed very difficult at the time, in retrospect, it is now clear that reaching an agreement with the customers was the easy part. The real work started when each party had to enroll support in undertaking fundamental business model transformation within their respective organizations. Establishing Digital Health capabilities provided its own unique set of learnings. While the team successfully launched a few commercial initiatives, breaking silos between different functions including medical affairs, pharmacovigilance, regulatory, legal, compliance, marketing, sales, and business development to create a cohesive team that could successfully and compliantly create new types of solution offerings was an undertaking by itself. The lessons learned, the "battles" fought, successes achieved, and failures encountered in establishing a Business Innovation function continue to form the basis for our deliberations on the barriers and opportunities for incumbents to break free from their past practices to invent a new future.

Innovation Is Not a Choice

Based on our experience, we have come to realize that innovation is not a matter of choice. However, the speed with which organizations recognize that things have changed and the manner with which they respond to define and address what innovation means for them *is* a critical choice linked intimately to long-term viability. While the case for innovation is usually clear, sometimes born out of a burning platform from which there is no other escape and other times arising from a fleeting glimpse of a new opportunity, there are many perceived barriers to innovation. Typically, these barriers, especially in entrenched incumbents that are industry leaders, can be attributed to human factors.

The most significant paradox is that the incumbents of today, certainly in the biopharmaceutical industry but also in other sectors, were the most prolific innovators of yesterday. However, as they transformed from innovative start-ups or faced multiple waves of disruption on their way to becoming industry-leading companies, the culture and mindset typically shifted from innovation to efficiency and cost management oriented toward delivering consistent financial performance over time. In the face of disruptive change, the status quo can become almost paralyzing. It becomes a big ask to shift the mission, purpose, culture, and associated operating model and business practices at incumbents. Examining new definitions and avenues of innovation beyond the accepted status quo requires courage seldom found in the management ranks typically comprised of individuals who have driven and observed success through a proven and entrenched model. Nor are the incentives structured to encourage such experimentation.

Furthermore, in the near term, traditional business is always more profitable. Why kill (or even maim) the goose that lays the golden eggs? Return on Investment (ROI) of "the new" is never clear, and metrics such as Net Present Value (NPV) and strategic optionality lose when the ROI of current business is high and proof of commercial principal in new initiatives is not fully developed. Resources are typically constrained, and there is a constant need to establish and review priorities. There is a need to sustain the current business and finding a balance between operating the current business and investing in new business "options" is not easy. Given a choice to invest the next dollar in sustaining the current business—for example by strengthening lobbying activities in Washington D.C. or finding new ways to find and engage patients—versus investing in experimentation that has unclear results, sustaining the current business typically wins. The pressure from the investment community focused on returns today does not make it easy to make such alternative investments. As Dr. David Feinberg, CEO of the Geisinger Health System, said, "the master of the biopharmaceutical industry is Wall Street and quarterly earnings reports."

The talent pool within biopharma incumbents, while typically highly qualified, intelligent and competent, is often not geared toward thinking beyond the current business. The leadership is mainly comprised of people who succeeded in revenue-generating roles under the current model—and it is challenging for most leaders to reinvent themselves. The culture of inertia and human factors prevails. Self-preservation creates barriers to self-disruption. Sunk costs in R&D establishment continue to create obstacles to non-traditional innovation. Performance incentives that are typically focused on revenue today versus longer term longevity of the business also add to the complexity.

These factors continue to limit the definition of innovation in the industry to the next biopharmaceutical product that can be packaged and sold as a pill or a vial for injection. In some cases, the transformation of the supporting product development and commercialization model, while important, is liberally characterized as innovation. The industry is lulled into a sense of comfort, and in the absence of a significant regulatory disruption to the industry's business model triggered by an economic meltdown or regulatory action, they may be right—in the near term. The risk the industry faces is that it may be caught "with its pants down" if such disruption happens. In the meantime, both the workforce and society are paying the price. The workforce continues to shrink with a constant focus on cost reductions to protect profitability, and society continues to bear a higher cost for incremental or marginal innovation.

As we defined earlier, innovation in the business context is about developing new products and services that generate new revenue streams. Investment in new sources of innovation to replace the declining value proposition of current products or services must be a matter of deliberate choice. Take for example the armed forces of the world. Countries are not continually fighting wars. However, they prepare endlessly for that disruptive event that could happen anytime, by investing in and training their armed forces, so they are not caught by surprise when that disruption occurs. Winners and losers are determined by the quality and strength of the armed forces. In the meantime, many innovations within the armed forces have spawned entire new commercial businesses. Aviator sunglasses initially developed to protect test pilots from the bright sunshine at high altitudes have become a commercial success. Jeep was initially designed as a light reconnaissance vehicle for the army and sold as a commercial vehicle after World War II. The aerosol was first invented to provide an easy mechanism to kill mosquitos, to protect U.S. soldiers stationed in the South Pacific from malaria. The technology, since improved, is now used extensively to deliver everything from medicines to sunscreens. In 1961, the U.S. Navy launched its first nuclear-powered aircraft carriers that could sail for long durations. However, given that human blood only has a 3-week shelf life, the Navy commissioned a team of doctors to see if they could figure out ways to store blood for longer durations. It was the experiments related to the development of long-shelf-life, reconstitutable hemoglobin that ultimately led to the understanding of angiogenesis and discovery of angiogenesis inhibitors such as Avastin and Nexavar that form the core of many cancer treatments today. The Internet came out of the defense industry and has enabled the human race to make disruptive leaps in every aspect of life over the last 30 years. Drones, another invention of the army, are now being considered to drop your medicines at your home.[7]

Similarly, building innovation capabilities and investing in diverse sources of innovation is a choice. It is a way to prepare, and develop muscle memory, so when that disruption occurs, you are ready to blaze new futures. One can't precisely time the disruptive event. However, survival beyond the event is determined by the long-term vision of preparing today. Along the way, the returns on innovation investment could be plenty. The fundamental questions then become:

- How do we change our mindsets to think in a bipolar fashion—rapidly and seamlessly toggling back and forth between today and the future?
- How do we align talent to create a long-term competitive advantage?
- How do we protect our future and build new ones?
- How do we best align these principles with an articulated vision for the entire organization communicated consistently and frequently, starting with the top (a key factor articulated by several of our external contributors)?

Our collective experiences in establishing a Business Innovation agenda and organization shaped the way we challenged our thinking on all of these factors. It all starts with having a clear innovation purpose and plan executed under the principles embodied by the 80-80 Rule.

Endnotes

1. "Humana and Boehringer Ingelheim Establish Partnership to Promote Population Health," March 25, 2013, accessed January 19, 2018, http://press.humana.com/press-release/humana-and-boehringer-ingelheim-establish-partnership-promote-population-health
2. "Boehringer Ingelheim, WellPoint and HealthCore Announce First Project Under Multi-Year Research Collaboration," November 14, 2014, accessed January 19, 2018, http://ir.antheminc.com/phoenix.zhtml?c=130104&p=irol-newsArticle&ID=1989824
3. "Boehringer Ingelheim and Sutter Health Establish Research Collaboration to Improve Patient Care," May 11, 2015, accessed January 19, 2018, https://news.sutterhealth.org/2015/05/11/boehringer-ingelheim-and-sutter-health-establish-research-collaboration-to-improve-patient-care/
4. "Anthem, HealthCore and Boehringer Ingelheim Initiate World's Largest Pragmatic Clinical Trial to Study People Living with COPD in a Real-World Setting," October 05, 2017, accessed January 19, 2018, https://www.businesswire.com/news/home/20171005005265/en/Anthem-HealthCore-Boehringer-Ingelheim-Initiate-World%E2%80%99s-Largest
5. "First Data from Boehringer Ingelheim, Anthem and HealthCore Multi-Year Study Show Gaps in Non-valvular Atrial Fibrillation Care," November 14, 2016, accessed January 19, 2018, https://www.boehringer-ingelheim.us/press-release/first-data-boehringer-ingelheim-anthem-and-healthcore-multi-year-study-show-gaps-non
6. "Propeller Health and Boehringer Ingelheim Announce New Partnership Focused on Improving Adherence and Care Management for People Living with COPD and Asthma," March 23, 2016, accessed January 19, 2018, https://www.propellerhealth.com/2016/03/23/

propeller-health-and-boehringer-ingelheim-announce-new-partnership-focused-on-improving-adherence-and-care-management-for-people-living-with-copd-and-asthma/

7. Evan Comen, *"15 commercial products invented for the military,"* *24/7 Wall St.*, June 06, 2017, accessed January 19, 2018, http://www.msn.com/en-us/money/companies/15-commercial-products-invented-for-the-military/ar-BBBJz2W

Chapter 4

Innovation Redefined

"If you want something new, you have to stop doing something old."

Peter F. Drucker

As we have noted, innovation in the industry typically refers to research, discovery, and development (R&D) of synthetic molecules or biological prescription drug products (pills, injections, and infusions), traditionally referred to as ethical biopharmaceuticals. We have made a case that continuing to invest in biopharmaceutical innovation with an almost exclusive focus on new molecules, whether early-stage discovery or late-stage development, will not fully capitalize on the opportunities to accelerate real advances in healthcare, and in fact, may lead to biopharmaceutical industry disruption. Overcoming inertia to preserve the status quo within most organizations requires that C-level leadership (including in some circumstances Board-level intervention) needs to deliberately re-define innovation and establish a clear agenda to drive the future of the companies and the industry. Marcus Wilson, President of HealthCore, agrees that many organizations struggle to think about how to innovate in business areas outside their historical success. This behavior is natural to some degree, but if it prevents the organization from moving forward, it could even be thought of as the "Tyranny of the Core."

Multiple frameworks in the current business literature discuss various types of innovation that can be useful in developing an innovation agenda. While the terms "pill," "pill plus," and "beyond the pill" have become very popular in healthcare, a *Harvard Business Review* paper "Managing Your Innovation Portfolio" by Bansi Nagji and Geoff Tuff[1] introduces the concept of Core, Adjacent, and Transformational Innovation. Core innovation is defined as optimizing existing products for existing customers; adjacent innovation refers to expanding from company business into "new to the company" business; transformational innovation refers to developing breakthroughs and inventing things for markets that don't yet exist. Drawing from an analogy from life in the Middle Ages, another approach is grounded in the terms "castles" and "ships," where castles represent the current business that needs to be defended (aka core), and ships represent an exploration of new opportunities (aka adjacent and transformational innovation). Other articles discuss innovation that is product-focused or service-focused. There is also discussion on business models that are based on either products, services, or platforms.

With this background, it is essential to understand that within the biopharma industry, there are two critical barriers to redefining innovation beyond the molecule:

■ The first is the perceived limitation to financial returns in areas beyond the traditional biopharmaceutical product, coupled with the belief that the current business model will continue to deliver as in the past. While this may be true in the near term (next 10–20 years), without a deliberate investment in alternative approaches with clear milestones and metrics to measure success, any attempts to innovate beyond the molecule will be fruitless. Ironically, in traditional R&D focused on product innovation in the industry, investments are routinely made based on assumptions on either return on investment (ROI) or net present value (NPV). At times, investments are also made to understand strategic options. Despite the fact that ROI and NPV calculations are based purely on speculative assumptions and rarely accurate, the comfort level of the industry in believing in biopharmaceutical product innovation is so entrenched that it is almost taken as fact relative to the perceived risk associated with new sources of innovation due to lack of alternative experience.

■ The second factor relates to lack of experience by most incumbents with non-product businesses. Over the last 150 years, the industry has earned its income by developing, marketing, and selling a well-defined product to the healthcare industry and patients with a well-defined use-case. To suddenly transition from a historically successful traditional biopharmaceutical product-based revenue model to a different product or even a service-based revenue model would require a significant transformation in internal talent and capabilities of the biopharmaceutical industry and may not be necessary. However, we can already see that evolving customer expectations regarding demonstration of value might be needed in, for example, an outcomes-based reimbursement model where the real-world performance of products matters more than what was demonstrated in the randomized clinical trials. Preparing to succeed in such a market environment will require the development of capabilities more aligned with a service industry focus. Looking at it from a global perspective, while the pressure to demonstrate value might be highest in the United States and European Union countries, there still seems to be a market for the traditional product in the mass markets of the developing world. However, given that 45% of industry revenues come from the U.S. market (with Japan a distant second at 9%), the ultimate need to transition to the broader innovation portfolio that generates new sources of revenue may not be a matter of choice.

Advocating for a broader innovation agenda for the industry should not translate into diversification for its sake. There are multiple initiatives within the biopharmaceutical industry aimed at getting into disease management, care management, population health management, or even the healthcare delivery space that have failed due to the limits on internal talent to launch adequately in these areas and a near term lack of proof of commercial value. Understanding these barriers, we do not support a complete transformation of the industry and abandoning its historical business model right away. We also do not advocate straying too far out of the core business of a "product" to treat diseases and not leveraging the core strengths the industry has. On the contrary, being excellent in fully leveraging and capitalizing on the revenue potential of the core provides the funding and competencies for expanding into new areas of innovation for incumbents who have the foresight to look beyond return on current investment. We propose that the industry prepares itself to transition into a health outcomes-focused, product-enabled services industry in the long term. Such a transformation will require a combination of product innovation expertise and consumer service mindset.

Redefining Innovation

Dr. David Rhew, Chief Medical Officer and Head of Healthcare and Fitness from Samsung Electronics America, is following the field closely and has observed that the biopharmaceutical industry is beginning to leverage digital health technologies, and in some cases, acquiring medical device companies to enhance their capabilities. Dr. Rhew believes that the rising costs of managing complex, chronic diseases may be a trigger to accelerate new developments. He sees an opportunity for biopharma to play a vital role in combining drugs and technology-supported behavioral modifications to increase adherence and improve the consistency of outcomes, which might lead to new business models.

Other healthcare innovators we spoke with are seeing the intersection of the more traditional biopharmaceutical industry and the rapidly emerging field of Digital Health on a daily basis. A common theme relates to the belief that while there are significant opportunities for creative partnerships, this sentiment is coupled with a caution that there are pitfalls for industry incumbents to avoid in rushing too quickly to invest in new technologies that may be over-hyped. Wearables, phone apps, and personal health records are cited as examples of technology that have not yet reached their full potential in operational readiness and commercialization. Some experts predict that the next ten years will make or break many organizations and see the emergence of new players in the healthcare ecosystem that may arise as hybrids comprised of today's fragmented components.

It is essential that every company determines both the right balance between the various components of its innovation strategy and the right timing for transformation given risk tolerance, urgency, and corporate culture. To enable a transformation of this magnitude, we advocate a process and a framework which would allow a step-wise transition of the biopharmaceutical industry from a "product" industry to a "health outcomes-focused, product-enabled services" industry. Adapted from "Managing Your Innovation Portfolio" by Bansi Nagji and Geoff Tuff[2] as it embodies the principles of various frameworks we discussed earlier, the proposed structure is three-dimensional:

> ***Drive the Core Business***. Invest in the process- and revenue-model innovation focused on driving efficiency, speed-to-market, and sustainability of the current business model linked to biopharmaceutical products.

Invest in Adjacent Innovation. We would like to
introduce a new industry sub-sector which we call,
Smart integrated Medicine or S[i]M. S[i]M encompasses
any medical intervention that is a combination of a
chemical molecule/biologic and a digital chip/other
digital technology capable of capturing and transmitting
data related to the body's physical, chemical, or
biological processes. S[i]M could come in many forms
characterized by route of administration, combined with
a biopharmaceutical product or a stand-alone personal
health management system agnostic to any other
component. Success with S[i]M would be enabled by
leveraging product-focused innovation capabilities of the
biopharmaceutical industry.

Additional adjacent value proposition could include
full participation in value-based care enabled by
S[i]M. Additionally, non-traditional monetization of
core assets can also generate new, adjacent revenue
streams.

Experiment with Breakthrough Innovation. Focus
on creating new business models based on learnings
from the adjacent innovation initiatives, for example,
S[i]M enabled services focused on delivering "Zero
Downtime for Patients." Incumbents today typically
think of discovery and development of new molecules
as breakthrough innovation. It is worth highlighting
that we are proposing a new definition of breakthrough
innovation that encourages investigation of new products,
services, or business models different from the traditional
biopharmaceutical product. We have taken the position
that traditional molecule-based innovation is the core
business of the incumbent biopharmaceutical industry,
and therefore can't be considered breakthrough anymore.
In our view, S[i]M, combined with the concept of Zero

Downtime for Patients, would form the foundation of a new industry sub-sector of the future.

In our view, applying the investment principles from current R&D practices—an ROI metric to core innovation investments, an NPV metric to adjacent innovation investments, and a Strategic Options metric to breakthrough investments—provides leadership with a proven way to invest and measure return on such efforts. It also provides a framework for managing resource allocation in a disciplined way. This approach supports leveraging the current core capabilities in the near term to create adjacent businesses and new skills and using those abilities to develop breakthrough businesses. At the same time, we also emphasize that the value of soft metrics such as strategic learning, capability building, and cultural change that is required for the industry to move beyond the molecule should not be underestimated. Lastly, if executed well, adjacent and breakthrough innovation initiatives could, in the long-term, become the core business of incumbents.

We propose an illustrative innovation opportunity map along the dimensions of Driving the Core, Investing in Adjacent, and Experimenting with Breakthrough next in Figure 4.1. The goal here is to trigger the thought process and start a conversation. Also, while this illustrative framework has been developed from an industry perspective, each company in the sector can use this structure to create a specific innovation portfolio that harnesses their organization's core competencies, selects the level of investments in various types of innovation based on organizational priorities, and is fit for purpose. Some may see this as a limited approach geared toward incremental, pragmatic transformation. However, as we will discuss later, this framework may allow new entrants to create an entirely new industry that can disrupt the current business model of the traditional biopharmaceutical industry.

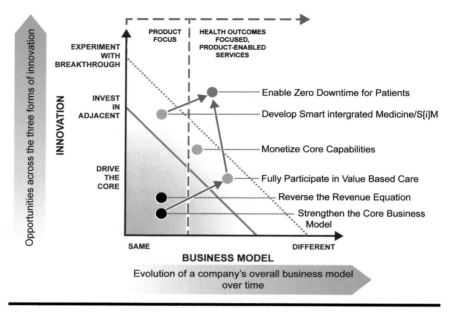

Figure 4.1   Illustrative opportunity map.

The Y-axis displays opportunities across the three forms of innovation described in the prior section. The X-axis displays the evolution of a company's overall business model over time which encompasses where and how it generates revenue and the way it interacts with the market through its customer engagement or commercial model. Additionally, while the boundary between the core and adjacent innovation initiatives is definite, the boundary between adjacent and breakthrough innovation initiatives tends to be permeable.

Drive the Core, but Know It Is a Short-Term Game

Focusing on strengthening and protecting the core value proposition for the foreseeable future is absolutely essential to generate the cash flow needed to fund future business models. In fact, as most biopharma companies transform, they continue to make investments in fine-tuning the current development and commercial model. We see the following two broad categories of innovation to drive the core value proposition the biopharma industry offers today.

1. ***Strengthen the Core***
   Global biopharma industry sales are projected to reach $1.85 trillion by 2019.[3] Based on this estimate, we can calculate that each additional month of exclusivity in the market can add approximately $150 billion to the revenue line. There are opportunities to fine-tune the entire development and commercialization model to drive speed to market, reduce costs to generate additional investment funds, and secure competitive advantage. Developing and executing an innovation strategy and portfolio of initiatives linked to optimizing the core can also serve as a learning laboratory for broader innovation opportunities on a platform that is tangible and familiar to current employees. Furthermore, it can identify those individuals in the organization who are willing and able to try new approaches that can be leveraged. Today, most biopharma companies are actively engaged in harnessing innovation to drive speed to market, which is an excellent first step. Applying the principles of the 80-80 Rule to push the boundaries of the core will be critical when it comes to the willingness to experiment, making decisions in the face of information gaps and taking risks across the enterprise. Examples include:
   - Applications of Artificial Intelligence (AI) and machine learning in the research phases can lead to a more cost-efficient discovery of viable products.
   - Use of digital technologies in the conduct of clinical trials could drive not only cost-efficiency, but also process efficiency that can drive speed to market. Further, such technologies enable engagement with

patients early on in a more active and involved manner than merely as test subjects, which can create targeted populations for subsequent involvement upon product launch. Blockchain could ensure robustness of remote clinical trials. Lastly, given the advent of digital therapeutics, becoming adept at conducting clinical trials on software or digital tools as therapeutics can only be a source of competitive advantage in the future.

- The industry has observed a decrease in individual practitioners and unaffiliated small group practices and diminished the effectiveness of the sales rep. In response, account-based selling models augmented with virtual detailing, working with patient advocacy groups to inform patient choice, and targeted advertising through electronic and social media, are all examples of pull-through innovation applied to the current commercial model.

- Going one step further, investments such as predictive analytics overlaid on claims or electronic medical records, patient engagement models focused on behaviors and motivations, investments in driving efficiencies in medication delivery, and participation in remote monitoring, all have the opportunity to grow pools of appropriate target patient populations. Pragmatic Clinical Trials (PCTs) could provide comprehensive insights related to the real-world performance of marketed products that can be utilized to improve patient experience, drive medication adherence, and inform future research.

While the list is not exhaustive, such initiatives can be fundamental to sustaining the core value proposition of biopharmaceutical products. In fact, most leading biopharmaceutical companies today are experimenting with or investing in such efforts; and in some cases, at the right scale.

2. *Reverse the Revenue Equation*

The fundamental basis of biopharmaceutical pricing that supports the core business model of incumbent biopharmaceutical companies has historically been linked to maximizing price in a small number of markets. Given that the volume of target populations eligible for approved indications is relatively fixed (setting aside opportunities to improve diagnosis or shorten time to onset of therapy), the focus, especially in the United States, has been on maximizing price, leveraging the employer-based insurance system and market-driven pricing mechanisms. Key determinants of price have included comparable products; other healthcare costs avoided, discounts and rebates projections based on coverage, the period of market exclusivity, and a desired profit margin accounting for the cost model. So far, the United States, even though it represents only 7% of the world's population, has accounted for approximately 45% (USD 450 billion) of global biopharmaceutical sales.[4] However, as biopharma pricing is under increasing scrutiny in the United States, the industry may want to consider reversing the emphasis on the revenue equation to one that focuses on maximizing volume by re-examining total market potential via a strategy that seeks to capture a broader global penetration (Figure 4.2). This approach would require being present earlier in geographies where today products are not launched until market exclusivity in the United States and other developed markets expires. By harnessing the global volumes, biopharma companies should be able to maximize the revenues at standardized global pricing and also potentially sustain current profitability levels estimated at 21%.[5]

We understand that this idea may trigger objections because in many countries the price may be capped by

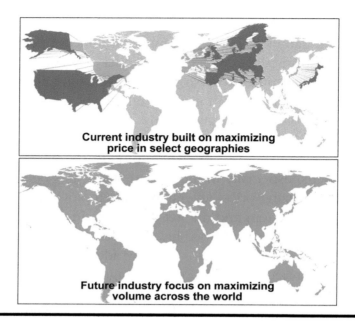

**Current industry built on maximizing
price in select geographies**

**Future industry focus on maximizing
volume across the world**

Figure 4.2　Reverse the revenue equation.

regulating bodies, and "reference pricing" has traditionally led
to product launch sequencing to protect prices in higher price
markets. However, as the individual economies are growing
the portion of budgets allocated to healthcare expenditure is
increasing, there could be room for negotiation for a standard
global price that allows access to innovative medicines to
much larger populations. Alternatively, given the level of price
transparency that exists today, manufacturers may just have
to get more comfortable setting and defending multiple price
points linked to the relative ability to pay, which will vary by
the local economic conditions.

For example, infectious diseases continue to be a
significant threat to world populations to varying degrees. In
the developed world, the primary concern is the emergence
of microbial strains resistant to commonly available and
sometimes overused treatments. In the developing world, the
concerns are more often grounded in poor sanitation and lack
of broad availability of even the most basic treatments. Global

populations are at risk, and governments are concerned about significant outbreaks. Given it is a universal public health concern, responding to this challenge via non-traditional commercialization strategy for antibiotics could be an area whereby applying the principles of the 80-80 Rule (fit for purpose), the idea of reversing the revenue equation, could be tested by offering the same price globally. At a minimum, taking a two-step approach where a single price is offered to a country or a group of nations first could be a good start. In the developed world, the higher price point for new treatments could be linked to costs avoided in managing resistant infections. In the developing world, the sheer volume of opportunity would suggest a lower price model or a bundled payment model with a blended price for both the new and older treatments proportional to need for a given population. By offering a single price in developed countries and a different single price in developing world countries, the concept of Reversing the Revenue Equation could be tested for impact on overall margins. Especially in the United States, it would be great to experiment if by offering a single price, costs related to differential pricing could be avoided and target margins potentially achieved by making medication available to all patients, insured or not, at the same price.

Invest in Adjacent; It Is Easier to Execute

Evidence of investments in adjacent innovation can also be found in the biopharma industry today. While not widespread or always driven by a defining purpose, companies are beginning to experiment with new services and solutions they can start to offer in the market. We provide examples of adjacent innovation illustrating how the biopharmaceutical industry can leverage its current core competencies and begin to play in spaces beyond the traditional biopharmaceutical product.

Smart integrated Medicine or S[i]M

We introduced the concept of Smart integrated Medicine or S[i]M earlier. In our view, S[i]M represents an adjacent product-based innovation in the context of the biopharmaceutical industry that can cover a wide range of applications.

There are several examples of organizations both from within and outside the biopharmaceutical industry that are already engaged in the development of new products, solutions, or approaches that could fall under the S[i]M framework:

A. In 2016, British Airways filed a patent titled "Travel Environment Control." The patent application includes a potential for "Digital pills or other ingestible sensors that detect internal temperature, stomach acidity, and other internal properties, and wirelessly relay this information outside the passenger's body."[6] The idea is to provide the cabin crew information on passenger comfort while traveling and alerting them when passengers need anything from water to food to blankets. The goal is to provide unparalleled service experience to its passengers (Figure 4.3).

B. Otsuka Pharmaceuticals, in partnership with Proteus Healthcare, has developed Abilify MyCite—a combination of 'Otsuka's now off-patent antipsychotic Abilify and Proteus's ingestible sensor that can help track medication ingestion, to help drive adherence and potentially improve management of psychiatric care. The FDA initially rejected the combination product in April 2016 on concerns related to patient safety and effectiveness under conditions of likely use, requesting additional human factor investigations. The companies refiled their application with required data in May 2017 and received final FDA approval in November 2017. Abilify MyCite

Figure 4.3   Real-time feedback becomes routine.

    is the first "Digital Medicine System" of its kind now available in the market.

C. While we were at Boehringer Ingelheim, the company signed an agreement with Qualcomm to develop a prototype for a smart sensor that could be embedded in the medication delivery device that the company uses for its respiratory products. The idea was that Qualcomm would develop a "prototype for a small, wireless, low-power, disposable module for the RESPIMAT inhaler. This fully-integrated inhaler… will be able to track actuations from the RESPIMAT inhaler, and the collected information can be shared with healthcare providers and people who have been prescribed one of Boehringer Ingelheim's RESPIMAT medicines and/or caregivers if more appropriate… with the goal of improving adherence to daily medicines that treat symptoms of COPD."[7]

    Other biopharmaceutical companies (and healthcare players outside pharma) are beginning to embrace the opportunities associated with digital enhancement of current diagnostic and therapeutic capabilities. The President of Lilly's U.S.

business and global diabetes franchise has recently indicated the commitment to participate in diagnostics and ways to monitor product performance versus just being a supplier of medications. Express Scripts, one of the three largest pharmacy benefit managers, recently announced an initiative to apply its clinical pharmacists to analyze and work with data generated by Propeller Health's technology that works with pulmonary delivery devices agnostic of the pharmaceutical product. Research in developing "Digital Markers" akin to biomarkers in identifying disease and treatment protocols is gaining speed.

There is also growing evidence of the efficacy of gaming, applications, coaching, and other non-biopharmaceutical interventions in managing diseases generated through studies mirroring randomized clinical trials. Companies like Omada Health have built successful businesses in the space, while companies like Samsung and Onduo continue to invest further.

There is the opportunity for the biopharmaceutical industry to leverage its core strengths in biopharmaceutical product development, obtaining regulatory approvals and commercialization to own the S[i]M space, either in combination with the molecule or without. The industry today monetizes its label that includes FDA-approved data on the safety and efficacy of the underlying product generated through randomized clinical trials. Leveraging its vast knowledge of diseases and embedding technology that can help measure the real-world effect in the human body is not only the smart thing, but also the right thing to do in advancing the value proposition and enabling opportunities to enter into new types of payment models.

My (Ruchin's) father has been managing a chronic disease with a fixed dose medication. An engineer by training, he experiments with the dose to avoid the side effects of the drug, in this case, severe headache, on a daily basis. And he is in constant search for alternatives because of that side effect.

Wouldn't it be great if every product came with technology that could help with "smart dosing," monitoring exactly how much medication you need and releasing it at the right time in the right amounts, so it minimizes side effects, which is one of the leading causes of medication non-adherence? Wouldn't that drive better adherence, healthy behaviors, and an overall reduction in the cost of care? Shouldn't the next patent application filed be not about "Extended Release" but "Appropriate Release?" There is a growing body of research on the multi-factorial basis for poor adherence beyond what most people focus on, namely cost. Concerns over side effects and not believing or accepting that patients need to be on the product in the first place (especially for non-symptomatic conditions) are high on the list. Technology that can bridge the information gap and create a more personalized connection between the patient and their treatments is likely to improve engagement and outcome.

In the automobile industry, once a generation of cars is launched—let's say the current-generation of Ford Explorer— for many years the underlying product platform, the chassis, the shape, the size of the car does not change. However, every year, feature sets like engine size, the color of the upholstery, the shape of headlights, and software gets updated. It allows the auto industry to continue to charge for that incremental innovation. Imagine a biopharmaceutical product where the underlying molecule is the same, but the "software" gets updated every year based on the real-world performance of last year? Yes, the FDA will need to evolve, but we have seen no indication that it is not willing to. One could even imagine that the price of the digitally-enabled product (or better yet the health improvement outcome associated with using the product) could change over time at the population or individual level based on updating the knowledge base with real-world experience.

As automobiles continue to evolve to become self-driving machines, SAE International standard J3016 defines six levels of automation for automakers, suppliers, and policymakers to classify the degree of automation sophistication.[8] We propose an analogous "RKJH 2018 Framework" that can be used to drive the evolution of the biopharmaceutical product from a static pill to S[i]M (Table 4.1). The framework can be adopted by manufacturers, payers, and regulators to innovate, regulate, and reimburse S[i]M systematically (Table 4.2).

Table 4.1   Smart Integrated Medicine or S[i]M

Any medicine that is a combination of a chemical molecule/biologic and a digital chip/other digital technology capable of capturing and transmitting data related to the body's physical, chemical, or biological processes. Smart integrated Medicine could come in many forms:
Smart implantable Medicine
Smart integrated Medicine that is implanted in the body
Smart ingestible Medicine
Smart integrated Medicine that is ingested orally
Smart injectable Medicine
Smart integrated Medicine that is injected in the body, either sub-dermally or into the bloodstream
Smart infusible Medicine
Smart integrated Medicine that is delivered via infusion
Smart inhalable Medicine
Smart integrated Medicine that is inhaled into the body
Smart involved Medicine
Smart integrated Medicine that is digital or digitally delivered in the absence of a biopharmaceutical product but still requires significant human involvement for it to exert its effect
Smart intercellular Medicine
Smart integrated Medicine that is applied topically to the skin, either as ointment or as a patch, and is delivered through intercellular pathways

Table 4.2   RKJH 2018 Standards to Define Levels of Smart integrated Medicine or S[i]M

RKJH 2018 Standards define levels of "Smart" features in **S[i]M** that can enable manufacturers, regulators, payers, providers, and patients to create approval, administration, and reimbursement policy frameworks and drive S[i]M's adoption and evolution.
Level 0: No Automation
Smart Capability: None.
Provider Involvement: Prescribing & administering.
Patient Involvement: Taking medication.
Biopharmaceutical Industry Involvement: Pharmacovigilance through spontaneous reporting.
Examples: All self or physician administered prescription products. E.g., pills, injections, infusions
Level 1: Passive Medication Adherence
Smart Capability: Passive Medication Reminders. Email or text-based alerts triggered by remote monitoring.
Provider Involvement: Prescribing, administering, monitoring & alerting.
Patient Involvement: Taking medication.
Biopharmaceutical Industry Involvement: Pharmacovigilance, adherence messaging, and monitoring at population level.
Examples: Smart Pill Bottles & Dispensers. E.g., AdhereTech, HERO, Livi@Home, Smart Inhalers (Propeller Health)
Level 2: Active Medication Adherence
Smart Capability: Medication reminders that alert patients when S[i]M concentration falls below a threshold within the body.
Provider Involvement: Prescribing, administering, and monitoring.
Patient Involvement: Taking S[i]M
Biopharmaceutical Industry Involvement: Pharmacovigilance.
Examples: Otsuka & Proteus Technologies combination product (Abilify + Smart Chip)

(Continued)

Table 4.2 (*Continued*)   RKJH 2018 Standards to Define Levels of Smart integrated Medicine or S[i]M

Level 3: Assisted Dosing
Smart Capability: S[i]M alerts patients and providers when medicine concentration falls below a threshold within the body, side effects and clinical efficacy and effectiveness.
Provider Involvement: Prescribing, administering, monitoring, and adjusting.
Patient Involvement: Taking S[i]M, adjusting regimen based on active engagement with provider.
Biopharmaceutical Industry Involvement: Enable Patient Provider Dialog. Active Recommendations. Pharmacovigilance.
Examples: None.
Level 4: Smart Dosing
Smart Capability: Automatic dose adjustment of S[i]M in body based on real-time monitoring and feedback of side effects, clinic efficacy and effectiveness.
Provider Involvement: Prescribing, administering, monitoring, and adjusting.
Patient Involvement: Taking S[i]M.
Biopharmaceutical Industry Involvement: Enable Patient Provider Dialog. Active Recommendations. Pharmacovigilance.
Examples: None.
Level 5: Healthy Time
Smart Capability: Maximizing potential of Levels 1–4, as appropriate.
Provider Involvement: Displaced as service provided by the biopharmaceutical industry, expanding the industry's footprint into traditional provider space
Patient Involvement: Taking S[i]M.
Biopharmaceutical Industry Involvement: Guarantee of healthy time through various levels of remote management. Pharmacovigilance.
Examples: None.

In addition, work being done by Virtual Physiological Human Institute to create the "Virtual Physiological Human (VPH)" could be transformative in its ability to conduct "clinical trials" for development of S[i]M. The Virtual Physiological Human is described as:

> "A European initiative that focuses on a methodological and technological framework that, once established, will enable collaborative investigation of the human body as a single complex system. The collective framework will make it possible to share resources and observations formed by institutions and organizations, creating disparate but integrated computer models of the mechanical, physical, and biochemical functions of a living human body."[9]

We believe the biopharmaceutical industry already has many of the required capabilities today, which if augmented with the right talent and investment, can take the industry on the path of S[i]M development. This first set of evolution would still keep it in the product innovation space but allow it to start to engage with patients in real time, understand the impact of medication in our bodies, drive medication adherence, and unleash research in the real world that can create future innovative products to improve human health. We can envision a future where the static label that is the basis for biopharmaceutical commercialization today evolves into a "dynamic label," where the properties of S[i]M related to the molecule remain constant. However, the associated digital technology evolves in real time based on individual patient feedback. In fact, recent FDA pre-certification of several companies involved in developing digital health products gives us confidence that such a future is not far away. In our view, the foundations of a new industry sub-sector, S[i]M, are already in place.

Full Participation in Value-Based Care

As we have noted, rapidly changing environmental factors driven mainly by unsustainable healthcare cost increases can create both challenges and opportunities for stakeholders across the healthcare ecosystem. Two significant trends include consolidation of both payers and providers, and a reduction in the willingness of payers (Centers for Medicare and Medicaid Services and private employers/insurers) to pay for volume versus outcome/value, both driving increased pricing pressure on the biopharmaceutical industry. Payment views are increasingly being shaped by law and regulation at both the federal and state levels under the PPACA or whatever may replace it. These challenges could be a threat for biopharma incumbents who are reluctant to move beyond their core business and commercial model, or an opportunity for those organizations that are willing to try a different approach. During our tenure at Boehringer Ingelheim the company chose to look at it as an opportunity and established the Organized Customer Collaborations initiative discussed previously. We found that the uncertainty being faced by all healthcare industry stakeholders regarding how to succeed could sometimes catalyze new types of conversations and potential partnerships. For sure, a more in-depth engagement between the biopharma company and payer/provider beyond what is feasible by sales representatives is needed. Biopharma companies seeking to participate in broader relationships must be willing to step back from their brands and engage in more open-ended discussions with payers and provider systems aimed at uncovering gaps in care which might be addressed by leveraging each parties' respective core capabilities.
An example would be collaborative research and jointly developed care management/improvement initiatives that can help demonstrate the appropriate role biopharmaceutical products (along with the research and extensive disease knowledge underpinning them) may play in improving the

health of patients. Additional benefits could include associated medical cost reductions, improvement in care delivery, or in key performance metrics such as Medicare Five-Star Quality ratings or Healthcare Effectiveness Data and Information Set (HEDIS) metrics, both of which have significant business implications for both payers and providers. Such collaborations can lead to new models for compensation based on outcomes and value (discussed later), or improved positioning on formularies and treatment guidelines (linked not only to the level of rebate paid, but also to the demonstration of mutually defined value), both of which will enhance the performance of the core business. More importantly, the collaborative dialog may also lead to the discovery of new opportunities that can be a source of adjacent revenue streams. Further, cross-industry partnerships could also allow all stakeholders to find ways to activate the value-based care system where it creates mutual value versus creating adversarial positions, and in turn benefit patients. In the absence of a deeper level of engagement, one could envision an adverse scenario for biopharma in which a third party takes responsibility for demonstrating and assuming the risk for the outcome. In such a situation, the branded biopharmaceutical product becomes merely an input which could be displaced by, for example, a generic or less expensive branded product in the same therapeutic class. S[i]M would enable biopharmaceutical companies to participate in value-based care as there will be verifiable data on the real-world outcome of the products that are managed by the biopharmaceutical industry and not a third party.

Non-Traditional Monetization of Core Capabilities

Another way to find new revenue streams is to identify the core capabilities a company has that can be offered to the market versus serving the inherent, core business model. Relevant examples may be found across industries.

Simon & Schuster, a renowned publisher, has, for example, created Archway Publishing, an independent publishing house that leverages Simon & Schuster's core capabilities of publishing best-selling books. However, rather than using the old business model of incurring the costs of publication upfront and then profiting from the sales and providing a share of earnings to the author, in the independent publishing space, the authors incur the upfront cost of publishing and share a portion of the sales with the publisher. By offering its core capabilities (book editing, designing, publishing, and marketing in the new format) and having the costs for these services paid upfront, Simon & Schuster has now created a new revenue stream.

Similarly, JLABS, an initiative of Johnson & Johnson, is an excellent example of adjacent innovation. JLABS describes its purpose as:

> "Our focus is on supporting emerging pharmaceutical, medical device, consumer, and digital health companies through the tenuous time between early discovery and having the necessary resources to move a product through the path to commercialization. We give companies every tangible advantage to succeed, providing access to core research facilities hosting specialized capital equipment, educational programs, operational capabilities, and a community of like-minded entrepreneurs. We also provide access to Johnson & Johnson Innovation deal teams expanding opportunities for venture capital funding, as well as the deal-making, therapeutic and technology area, product development, and commercialization expertise of Johnson & Johnson. Therapeutic areas of focus include oncology, immunology, neuroscience, cardiovascular and metabolism, infectious diseases, and vaccines."[10]

By creating JLABS, Johnson & Johnson has found a way to monetize the early discovery capabilities core to its biopharmaceutical business. Further, by offering the same infrastructure to early-stage entrepreneurs and companies, not only is it creating an upfront revenue stream in the form of fees to use the labs, but it has also created an incubator for external innovation that can generate the future pipeline of products and solutions for the business.

Can biopharma companies look at offering their clinical trials and regulatory approval expertise as a service to emerging biotech, digital health, and health and wellness companies to create evidence-based solutions? Can biopharma companies look at monetizing the vast amounts of disease-related data they own by making it accessible to researchers and entrepreneurs worldwide? Can biopharma companies offer sales training as a service to entities building sales forces?

In our mind, these initiatives will also prepare the biopharmaceutical industry to experiment with more "service-oriented" business models—an intermediary step to evolve into "product-enabled service-focused companies" of the future.

How will players from other healthcare sectors react to a broader role for biopharma? We tested this with several of our contributors. All are convinced that biopharma does, in fact, possess an in-depth knowledge of disease states, expertise in research, comprehensive analytics capabilities and some real success in changing behavior through its marketing initiatives. The reaction to seeing biopharma move into new areas based on these competencies varied considerably. One thought that payers and providers would not be comfortable with pharma getting closer to patient-level data and might even view them as competitors. However, another was very clear that pharma needs to be a full partner provided they are willing to look beyond individual biopharmaceutical products.

Experiment with Breakthrough to Define New Futures

Focus on Health versus Disease: Zero Downtime for Patients

At present, biopharma revenue is almost exclusively derived from direct product sales, yet it is the interaction between the product and the individual patient, that is, the therapeutic outcome, that delivers the ultimate value of the product. Due to the nature of population-based product development approaches based on averages, there is considerable variability in patient-level response including whether the product will work at all or deliver an acceptable safety profile. Furthermore, while the reaction to the product is sometimes apparent through readily available testing, for example, blood-pressure reduction or lipid-lowering, these are mainly surrogate end-points for a broader intended effect. As we have discussed before, there are increasing pressures to evolve the pricing model to one based on outcomes either at the patient or population level. This evolution could manifest in differential pricing linked to outcome, pay only upon demonstration of effect, upfront payment followed by differential rebates tied to outcome, credit for cost savings in non-pharma components of related healthcare costs or some combination thereof. The question for the biopharmaceutical industry is whether they are willing and able to develop or partner with other entities, to develop technology and methods to measure the outcome in a more meaningful way, and to enable more sophisticated payment models.

Many companies, from IBM to Netflix, are transitioning from product to service-based models. GE is looking to offer the guarantee of "zero unplanned downtime" for its customers by embedding software and analytics in the entire range of its industrial products—from the train to aircraft engines to turbines and washing machines. One future vision for the biopharmaceutical industry could be grounded in a product offering linked with a differential type of financing model based on "zero downtime" for patients. The product in this example could be a conventional pharmaceutical (or not) coupled with non-pharmacological technology that delivers a physiological and/or psychological effect measured via a self-contained feedback system to demonstrate impact at the individual patient level. The real sources of innovation could be the combination of different (and currently disconnected) technologies or the revenue generation model for the industry. In this case, the technology itself is not the revenue source but rather an investment to generate revenue tied to the outcome which could occur at an individual therapeutic area or disease level or at the level of overall patient health. In the ultimate extension of this model, generating revenue for a positive patient outcome in the complete absence of consumption of any pharmaceutical products would be a win.

While the biopharma industry is currently implementing outcomes-based contracts where an effect is easily identifiable and measurable, for example, prevention of hospital readmission within 30 days, or reduction in the hemoglobin A1C level in people with diabetes below a certain percentage within a given period, the payments are still tied to the product. In one of the latest examples, Novartis has offered the government of Japan to launch Kymriah, a cancer treatment based on an outcomes-based payment model where the company is paid only if no tumor cells are detectable a month after treatment. However, if an outcome is achieved, the payment is still linked to the product. Can we instead think of a future where the payments to the biopharma industry are not based on achievement of that one-time milestone, but on an overall measure of health the patient achieves based on that treatment (e.g., time of progression-free survival in the case of oncology products)? Can S[i]M enable the biopharmaceutical industry to engage patients by becoming a true partner in delivering health every minute of every day? Is it possible for the biopharmaceutical industry to achieve Level 5 of

RKJH 2018 Standards, where such a concept becomes a reality? The payment terms could then be structured as an annuity for as long as the patient lives, in contrast to payment received when a patient fills the prescription. As we discuss later, one of our contributors—the CEO of a nationally recognized Health System—sees the opportunity for companies to assume full risk for pharmaceutical-based care under a capitation model which could be a step along the journey toward "zero downtime" and a completely different payment and revenue model. Shifting the debate from the price/cost of biopharmaceuticals to the value of an integrated health outcome delivered should be a much more productive discussion for all parties.

Beyond Healthcare

Every day, there are stories of Amazon disrupting another industry. It started with how we buy books, then redefined retail and consumer goods industries, the media and entertainment industry, the grocery industry, and lately we hear about its entry into healthcare and even logistics, causing FedEx and UPS to take note. It has created a technology infrastructure business in cloud services, has launched Alexa—a combination of voice recognition and artificial intelligence engine as a virtual assistant—and allowed individual sellers to use its platform to sell their products for a commission. The story goes on. So, what is it about Amazon that enables it to expand in every conceivable industry? Some say that the fact that it is not held hostage to margin pressures by the street (in fact, it is still to report a profit and yet it remains one of the most highly recommended stocks in the market). As a result, it continues to invest in businesses of the future and continues to drive even higher return to its investors (both institutional and individual).

Should the biopharma industry disrupt its financial model and create an engine that allows it to play in various segments of healthcare? We believe the answer should be yes. But should the industry diversify beyond healthcare? We are not sure yet. We do not advocate building highly diversified conglomerates. There is enough debate in the literature on the advantages and disadvantages of conglomerates. On the one hand, they help diversify risk. On the other, they have a different investment return profile versus pure plays. In the near term, we recommend staying within healthcare—there is an immense opportunity there, and the industry has the capabilities to evolve itself to remain a vital value provider.

We see a few different types of conglomerates operating in the biopharmaceutical industry today. One type could be categorized as product-based conglomerates. For example, Johnson & Johnson operates in three healthcare product segments—Biopharmaceuticals, Medical Devices, and Over-the-Counter. Boehringer Ingelheim is active in Biopharmaceuticals, Biosimilars, and Animal Health. Novartis operates in Biopharmaceuticals, Eyecare, and Generics segments. A second type includes companies like Luye Life Sciences Group that has both a biopharmaceutical product and healthcare services focus seeking to leverage synergies and thereby offer end-to-end precision medical services ranging from diagnostics to treatment. A third type is represented by highly diversified conglomerates such as Samsung and GE which are active in the product (Biosimilars, Medical Devices) and service businesses (health technology, services). While we do not advocate incumbent biopharmaceutical players to become highly diversified conglomerates such as GE and Samsung, we do see value in adopting hybrid product and services business models similar to Luye to be able to capture more significant value in the broader healthcare market.

We have titled this chapter Innovation Redefined, a tall order for sure but we have described many ways for an incumbent organization to take up the challenge. Transforming the development and commercialization processes, adding incremental attributes to biopharmaceutical products that improve the overall customer experience, moving the payment model from paying for the product to paying for the outcome or value are all opportunities to innovate in the core. Applying digital technology capabilities to create S[i]M offers many ways to evolve into adjacent spaces. Breakthrough innovation for an individual organization can involve anything from monetizing existing internal capabilities with third-party customers to create new revenue streams to capturing value across the broader healthcare value chain by entering into creative partnerships with the goal of selling health versus individual products. The most important factor is to recognize that the past success is not sufficient to guarantee the future and to then take the initial steps to a new journey.

Endnotes

1. Bansi Nagji and Geoff Tuff, *"Managing Your Innovation Portfolio,"* Harvard Business Review, May 2012.
2. Bansi Nagji and Geoff Tuff, *"Managing Your Innovation Portfolio,"* Harvard Business Review, May 2012.
3. Deloitte. *"2016 Global Life Sciences Outlook. Moving Forward with Cautious Optimism,"* accessed January 19, 2018, https://www2.deloitte.com/content/dam/Deloitte/global/Documents/Life-Sciences-Health-Care/gx-lshc-2016-life-sciences-outlook.pdf
4. Statista, "U.S. Pharmaceutical Industry—Statistics & Facts," accessed January 19, 2018, https://www.statista.com/topics/1719/pharmaceutical-industry/
5. Keith Speights, *"12 Big Pharma Stats That Will Blow You Away,"* *The Motley Fool,* July 31, 2016, accessed January 19, 2018, https://www.fool.com/investing/2016/07/31/12-big-pharma-stats-that-will-blow-you-away.aspx
6. Chuck Martin, *"British Airways Could Give Passengers A 'Digital Pill',"* *MediaPost,* November 30, 2016, accessed January 19, 2018, https://www.mediapost.com/publications/article/290040/british-airways-could-give-passengers-a-digital-p.html

7. "Qualcomm and Boehringer Ingelheim Pharmaceuticals Collaborate to Add New Digital Technology to RESPIMAT® Inhaler," August 30, 2016, accessed January 19, 2018, https://www.qualcomm.com/news/releases/2016/08/30/qualcomm-and-boehringer-ingelheim-pharmaceuticals-collaborate-add-new
8. David Beard, *"Auto No Mo'Us,"* *Car and Driver,* November 2017, Page 71.
9. VPH Institute, "What Is the VPH?" accessed January 19, 2018, http://www.vph-institute.org/what-is-vph-institute.html
10. Johnson & Johnson Innovation, JLABS, accessed January 31, 2018, https://jlabs.jnjinnovation.com/about-us

Chapter 5

Next-Generation Unicorn Industry

"You never change things by fighting the existing reality. To change things, build a new model that makes the existing model obsolete."

R. Buckminster Fuller

Next-generation unicorn industry.

In the previous chapter, we proposed an innovation opportunity map that broadens the definition of innovation for the entire biopharmaceutical industry by encouraging it to explore innovation opportunities beyond the traditional biopharmaceutical product or associated business model. On a more proximal level, individual companies in the industry need to pragmatically adapt and iterate their respective innovation program based on internal competencies, willingness to take the risk, investment ability, and leadership affinity, among other factors. The proposed approach should not be viewed as a static recommendation. The idea is to challenge the traditional planning processes of the biopharmaceutical industry that can lead to the evolution of innovation thinking beyond the molecule-based biopharmaceutical products.

In our view, for the bellwether incumbents of the biopharmaceutical industry such as Pfizer, Johnson & Johnson, Novartis, and Sanofi, the challenge of finding an appropriate innovation agenda beyond the core business can be daunting, but they have the resources to explore the future at the right level of scale and investment. They need to seek a balance between maintaining current customer relationships and investor satisfaction linked to the existing core business while looking to the future where current and new business models are not necessarily an either/or choice. The trick is in finding the right balance between sustaining the current business model so that cost/revenue equilibrium can be maintained and investing in multiple new adjacent and breakthrough options to disrupt themselves over time.

In contrast, for early-stage companies, experimenting with the concepts of S[i]M and Zero Downtime for Patients represents a greenfield opportunity that could help them displace and disrupt the incumbents. It is an opening in time that holds the promise of creating the Next-Generation Unicorn Industry (Figure 5.1) aligned with the need and expectations of shifting generations where digital defines the

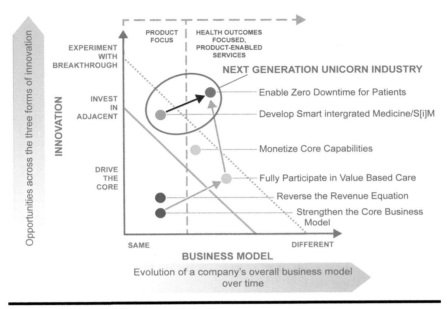

Figure 5.1   A greenfield opportunity to create a new industry?

collective consciousness and existential reality of a hybrid real and virtual day-to-day life.

To elaborate, the Greek polis is considered the quintessential model for the organization of public life. From the fifth century BC, the physical architecture of the Greek polis defined the physical ecosystem within which human activity, communications, and interactions happened. Over time, businesses studied these physical interactions to understand unmet needs they could fulfill (from food to transportation). Places of public gathering, such as markets and public squares became the places where political dialog as well as transactional activities including marketing, buying, and selling happened. While the Greek polis was an "oral" society defined by physical space,[1] with the advent of technological means of communications, our society today has become technology- based, and our new reality is a hybrid of physical and cyberspace (Figure 5.2).

While the Defense Advanced Research Projects Agency (DARPA) is responsible for the Internet of today, the word

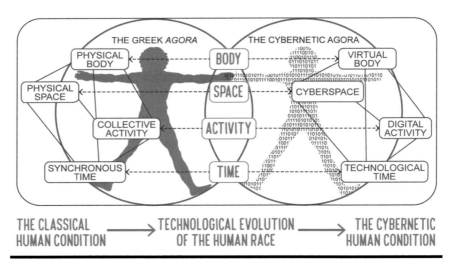

THE GREEK *AGORA*   THE CYBERNETIC AGORA

PHYSICAL BODY ← BODY → VIRTUAL BODY

PHYSICAL SPACE ← SPACE → CYBERSPACE

COLLECTIVE ACTIVITY ← ACTIVITY → DIGITAL ACTIVITY

SYNCHRONOUS TIME ← TIME → TECHNOLOGICAL TIME

THE CLASSICAL HUMAN CONDITION → TECHNOLOGICAL EVOLUTION OF THE HUMAN RACE → THE CYBERNETIC HUMAN CONDITION

Figure 5.2   Hybrid human existence. (Kansal, *The Contemporary Public Place*, Page 46.)

cyberspace comes from William Gibson's book, *Neuromancer* (1984. NY: Ace Books). He defined cyberspace as: "a unified conceptualization of space spanning the entire Net and [that] exists only as a consensual hallucination on the part of the hosts and users which participate in it." Cyberspace can simply be understood as the space that exists in the universal, networked environments of computers, smartphones, virtual reality, and other digital devices. In 1984 it was fiction, today cyberspace is as much a part of our daily existence as is the physical space. We have become techno-organic, digitally networked human beings that co-exist in a hybrid space. Facebook is a prime example of the parallel cyberspace we exist in today. It is the new Greek polis—the new agora. It is where we "go" on a daily basis to meet people, communicate, exchange information, have political dialog, and even conduct political espionage. It is where we are marketed to, advertised to, sold to. It is where we go for reviews, opinions, and consumption of news. It has become as much a part of our daily life as the Cartesian physical space we live in. And it has disrupted many traditional business models along the way.

In the pre-cybernetic age, healthcare was a purely physical endeavor, both from a delivery and interventions perspectives. As we become comfortable with consumption of information and experiences in our cybernetic existence, it creates opportunities for new ways of delivering and experiencing healthcare. From the healthcare delivery perspective, tele-consults (Teladoc), remote robotic surgeries (DaVinci), and virtual-reality-assisted surgeries are fast gaining ground. At the same time, from the healthcare products and treatments perspective, we are seeing digital interventions emerging to help manage diseases—it's the new world of "Digital Therapeutics." While Omada Health is thought to have coined the term to describe its online coaching platform for pre-diabetics to prevent disease, the idea is to have "software that can improve a person's health as much as a drug can, but without the same cost and side-effects."[2] It refers to the replacement of drugs by software. In September 2017, Pear Therapeutics announced that "it has received an Expedited Access Pathway (EAP) designation from the FDA for its reSET-O™ Prescription Digital Therapeutic, the first of its kind designed for treating Opioid Use Disorder (OUD)."[3] Big Health's "Sleepio"[4] is an alternative to sleeping pills. Virta Health, launched in 2017, is positioned as "an online specialty medical clinic that reverses type 2 diabetes without medications or surgery."[5] It is not outside of the realm of possibility that in our hybrid existence between physical and cyberspace, such digital therapeutics will become a mainstay in our medicine cabinets.

A breakthrough innovation in the context of the traditional healthcare ecosystem, digital therapeutics are taking advantage of the new, emerging hybrid ecosystem (physical and cyberspace). Digital therapeutics companies are developing simple, modular products that can be seamlessly distributed and consumed in this hybrid environment of human existence. In our view, S[i]M that can bridge the traditional molecule-based pill with emergent digital therapeutics will create a more holistic treatment experience that has the power to reposition the biopharmaceutical industry in the healthcare ecosystem.

As discussed earlier, RKJH 2018 Standards for S[i]M provide a blueprint for the biopharmaceutical industry to increase direct engagement with patients and assist with care management. The ability to predict and prevent illness, and to enable Zero Downtime for Patients, would afford the biopharmaceutical industry a new monetary opportunity that goes beyond the development and sale of a pill. However, the industry will need to develop a deep understanding of the new hybrid existential ecosystem in addition to the traditional biological and epidemiological knowledge of diseases to become successful. Harnessing its strengths in creating simple and modular solutions, it can then prevent commoditization and position itself for capturing broader value in the new, hyper-connected healthcare ecosystem. As affluence levels continue to increase globally and larger proportions of society can afford to move up the pyramid of Maslow's hierarchy of needs including an increased focus on health and well being; the biopharmaceutical industry can broaden the geographic basis of its profit and strive to become a Next-Generation Unicorn Industry.

We would be amiss if we did not address the concern around protection of privacy. The debate regarding invasions of privacy associated with the proliferation of digital technology and data capture in the context of hybrid human existence has reached a high tempo today. In our view, privacy concerns are highest when the transparency created especially by advancement in technology or regulation is a novelty. Once ubiquitous, such transparency becomes universally accepted part of life and contributes to the evolution of the human race.[6] We firmly believe in the inherent ability of society to continue to find the right balance between individual privacy and the larger good achieved through sharing of what may historically be considered private, and the resulting evolution of collective consciousness.

Paradoxically, the root of the word technology lies in the Greek word *techne,* which refers to the act of revealing, of bringing forth the truth, of creating transparency. In works of philosophy, the term *Vita Activa* is used to define human existence based on activities essential for the existence of human life—labor (refers to biological processes of human body—the cycle of procreation, life and death), work (refers to the production of artificial world of things), and action (refers to interrelationships between humans at community and political level). While in historical times it may have been possible to separate the *Vita Activa* along the rigid dichotomy of public and private, the boundaries have always been fluid and have undergone various mutations with the changing notions of human existence during the evolution of the human race: political, social, cultural, economic, and technological. In fact, Aristotle viewed public life as more important than the time spent in the household or individual existence, "since the whole is of necessity prior to the part." In his view, the very purpose of public existence was the contribution it made to progress toward a good life and happiness of individuals. He noted that "we must not suppose that any one of the citizens belongs to himself, for they all belong to the state and are each part of the state, and the care of each part is inseparable from the care of the whole." Philosophers such as Hannah Arendt argued that the singular, private human existence has no meaning devoid of interaction with other humans and an ability to transcend what is particular to oneself and engage in what is common to the species.[7]

Within this new reality of human existence, what will the biopharmaceutical industry and each of the individual companies transform into? We neither have all the answers, nor can we guarantee that the profit margins would be similar in the new spaces. We do see the promise and possibilities if the industry chooses to embrace concepts such as what we have called a S[i]M that can potentially broaden the industry's value proposition in the market, either driven by incumbents or new entrants. We can foresee a future where the question "Have you taken your medicine?" is replaced by "Have you taken your S[i]M?" If the incumbent biopharmaceutical industry does not rapidly transform, we believe it risks suffering a slow death through mergers and acquisitions, lack of pricing power, and ultimately lack of innovative products that meet rapidly evolving customer expectations.

We can also foresee a future where medical science and the regulatory framework has further evolved, capabilities of gene therapy are fully harnessed, and diseases are cured with a single intervention. One can envision a future where Zero Downtime for Patients becomes endogenous via integration of a modified genome from which deleterious genes have been removed or corrected into the primary human gene pool versus delivered through artificial interventions such as S[i]M. In that scenario, the concept of S[i]M will also become a relic of the past. While we can't foresee the industry's future in that scenario, we are confident that the disruption cycle will continue to accelerate and spawn the emergence of the next unicorn. In that spirit, we believe that an evolving innovation agenda must be seen as a fundamental component of helping prepare incumbents to anticipate and plan for any future.

Ultimately, no innovation agenda will be successful unless it is supported by a strong execution focus. In the next section, we discuss how applying the principles of the 80-80 Rule can reignite growth for the industry. We can virtually guarantee that bold, ambitious, alternative approaches will not be perfect the first time, but with the right focus, a culture of rapid experimentation and iteration inherent to the 80-80 Rule, they will yield results for the future.

Endnotes

1. Ruchin Kansal, *The Contemporary Public Place. Normative and Spatial Implications of Cyberspace on the Architecture of the Public Realm* (Kansas State University, 1997), Page 22.
2. Christina Farr, *"Can "Digital Therapeutics" Be as Good as Drugs?" MIT Technology Review,* April 7, 2017, accessed January 20, 2018, https://www.technologyreview.com/s/604053/can-digital-therapeutics-be-as-good-as-drugs/
3. "Pear Obtains FDA Clearance of the First Prescription Digital Therapeutic to Treat Disease," September 14, 2017, accessed January 20, 2018, https://peartherapeutics.com/category/press/
4. "Sleepio," accessed January 20, 2018, www.sleepio.com
5. "Virta," accessed January 20, 2018, www.virtahealth.com
6. Kansal, *The Contemporary Public Place.*
7. Kansal, *The Contemporary Public Place.*

IGNITING GROWTH

Chapter 6

Applying "The 80-80 Rule"

THE 80-80 RULE: BEING 80% CONFIDENT THAT YOU WILL ONLY BE 80% RIGHT THE FIRST TIME SHOULD FEEL NORMAL

- If you are 100% confident, you are not looking for blind-spots. This attitude borders on arrogance.
- If you wait to be 100% confident, it probably means that someone else may have already capitalized on your idea because you spent too much time in the quest for perfection.
- And if you are 100% right the first time, it is pure chance, not an act of genius.

SETTING UP FOR SUCCESS

FINDING WHITE SPACES

4 PRINCIPLES FOR IGNITING GROWTH

DEVELOPING NEW VENTURES

BECOMING ADEPT AT PARTNERING

Embracing the 80-80 Rule to ignite growth.

We hope that by now you have gained a deeper understanding of the opportunities and challenges faced by incumbent biopharmaceutical manufacturers as they address an unprecedented magnitude and rate of change across the healthcare ecosystem. As industry insiders, our effort has been to offer insights into how the industry has demonstrated success in serving as a beacon of innovation that most other industries can only dream about. This unwavering commitment to continuous innovation in the discovery and development of new biopharmaceutical products coupled with some unique legal and regulatory conditions gave rise to what we termed a Unicorn Industry.

However, we have also offered our view that some of the factors that contributed to the industry's historical success in its core business have inadvertently made it more difficult for it to innovate in other areas of healthcare. Areas that we have designated as adjacent or breakthrough; opportunities which may increasingly be co-opted by new players from outside the industry. We offer this provocative warning not as an indictment of industry incumbents' strategic choices or leadership failures but rather as a rallying cry to re-ignite the spirit of innovation that made the industry so successful in the past. It is our belief that bringing together the appropriate way of thinking about innovation in respective companies along with the "soft factors" embodied by the principles of the 80-80 Rule can get any organization off to a good start in igniting growth in both its historical core and new business opportunities.

We propose that the 80-80 Rule set the standard for redefining innovation to ignite growth in the incumbent biopharmaceutical industry and enable it to reclaim its rightful place as a driver of healthcare improvement.

Based on our experience in setting up for adjacent and breakthrough innovation, combined with an observational study of peer companies as well as companies in other industries, discussions with executive leadership across industry stakeholders, customers, analysts, and consultants, we propose the following building blocks that must be put in place:

Setting Up for Success
– Leadership Foresight and Courage to Invest
– A New Breed of Leaders
– Teaming the Right Talent
Finding White Spaces
– Embrace the Need, Money Will Follow
– Outside In First, Inside Out Next
Developing New Ventures
– Design for the End User, but Consider the Ecosystem
– Keep It Modular
– Keep It Simple
Becoming Adept at Partnering
– Partnerships that Span Development and Commercialization
– Making Partnerships Work

The Principles of the 80-80 Rule should be applied as companies invest in these building blocks. The 80-80 Rule emphasizes speed and willingness to embrace a degree of uncertainty, both of which must exceed that of the historical product discovery/development model of the biopharma industry. It advocates "fit for purpose" experimentation that must be adopted by the industry to prevent a slow demise or displacement from the healthcare value chain by disrupters from outside the industry. Taking new risks, being comfortable with uncertainty and challenging the status quo should feel normal again. Lastly, there is no substitute for flawless execution.

These principles are equally valid for new entrants that are looking to shape the industry's future or even create the new S[i]M subsector as we have proposed. In our minds, the original innovators and venture capitalists of the biotech industry represent a great example of embracing the tenets of the 80-80 Rule in spawning a highly successful industry subsector that quickly evolved from being viewed as speculative and risky to one that is now considered part of the mainstream industry. There is no reason why today's innovators, entrepreneurs, and venture capitalists could not similarly lead their respective firms to the development of a new S[i]M industry subsector.

Chapter 7

Setting Up for Success

We must pause and ponder if the industry needs a new breed of leadership that will shape its future.

Leadership Foresight and Courage to Invest

"History remembers kings and rulers—not ministers and the general population—for what defined the character of their times. It begins and ends at the top."

CEOs are kings of the modern world, and employees can be viewed as the royal advisors and the general population. If the CEOs don't lead with a vision and mandate and sponsor innovation efforts beyond the core, those initiatives will die on the vine.

Innovation beyond the core requires foresight. Innovation requires courage to invest. It requires a sustained level of investment over time for new initiatives to yield results. And there is no task more important for leadership than to find the right balance between the need to run the current core business effectively and to create space for adjacent and breakthrough innovation that may someday cannibalize the existing business. While investments in such adjacent and breakthrough innovations typically come with no immediate Return On Investment (ROI), if done at the right volume such investments almost always produce smart strategic options that either enhance revenue from current businesses, point the way toward new business opportunities, or become the new basis of profit for such companies. For example, early investments in cloud computing by Bill Gates allowed Satya Nadella at Microsoft to grow that business to be almost as big as the core operating system business (and ultimately rise to become the CEO). Similarly, investments in video streaming allowed Reed Hastings to transform Netflix from a DVD mail-order company to a streaming service omnipresent on all digital devices. Under Chairman Chen Wang, HTC is diversifying itself from a manufacturer of smartphones into the Internet of Things, fitness, and virtual reality. What is also noteworthy is that these companies have been in existence for only the last 40 years or less and are no longer in the original business that they created. On the other hand, companies from Kodak to Borders to Blockbuster—once the innovators and stalwarts of their industry—either did not foresee or chose to ignore the potential disruption to their core business and eventually declined because the investment in self-transformation was either too little or came too late.

As we have discussed, the biopharmaceutical industry has progressed through several waves of change throughout its history. It was driven by:

■ New business dynamics or market requirements;
■ Core technology availability (e.g., large-scale organic chemistry or biotechnology) supported by increased internal investment from within incumbents; and
■ External legal and regulatory forces which demanded incremental investment in capabilities just to stay in business and survive.

However, none of these illustrate the urgency that the industry faces today in freeing up additional investment outside of business as usual or responding to incremental requirements in the core.

Bansi Nagji and Geoff Tuff in their paper "Managing Your Innovation Portfolio" propose a Golden Ratio of 70-20-10: that is, 70% of investment in the core business, 20% in adjacent innovation, and 10% in breakthrough innovation. Coincidentally, they have found in their research that such investments yield a return of 10-20-70, that is, 10% from investments in the core, 20% from investments in adjacent, and 70% from investments in breakthrough innovation initiatives.[1] While we are not suggesting that every incumbent company use the Golden Ratio to build a balanced innovation portfolio, we do recommend a diversified one that goes beyond investments in traditional biopharmaceutical products as the basis for future sustenance and growth. The winners of the future will be characterized by those that can look beyond their historical successes.

When companies are highly profitable, and cash flow is not a problem, incremental investments in adjacent and breakthrough initiatives are easy to make as the pressure on margins and need to demonstrate immediate ROI is not as critical. For incumbents that are struggling with profit margins, such investments tend to get no air time because leadership stays focused on near term financial targets and doubles down on strategies that may have worked in the past. It will take courage, but are the incumbents willing to consider a new allocation of their R&D budget on core versus adjacent or breakthrough innovation, and establish new performance metrics that go beyond commercially successful molecule-based products to measure success?

While the best time to invest in innovation is when the business is robust, visionary leadership is especially critical in more challenging times. Embracing the 80-80 Rule demands that leaders become comfortable with funding and sponsoring concepts that are not fully developed or supported by rigorous ROI calculations grounded in past success. Those leaders may want to consider adopting a new vernacular for projects and initiatives that can be recognized as following the individual company's version of the 80-80 Rule regarding what is fit for purpose. Such a vernacular would help with positioning and would clarify steering and governance of the high-risk/high-reward component of their respective project portfolios.

A New Breed of Leaders

> "Do not follow where the path may lead. Go instead where there is no path and leave a trail."
>
> **Ralph Waldo Emerson**

We firmly believe that a successful innovation agenda in any organization starts and ends with the leadership. Difficult times need leaders that create space and investment in innovation for future growth. Such leaders allocate as much time and interest to innovation as they do to the core business. They own the innovation agenda and are change agents, not merely managers. They know that if they don't actively and visibly embrace this role, the path to organizational irrelevance accelerates.

Companies need to take a critical look at their talent development strategies to develop such change agents as their leaders. In the biopharmaceutical industry, given the perceived uniqueness of the business model, leadership is typically groomed from within over time. The leaders at the top have been highly successful in traditional disciplines—marketing, sales, R&D, finance, even legal. They are groomed to have global experience. They are good portfolio managers. They are also capable people leaders.

In a business environment characterized by disruption versus stability, should these leaders also be required to have significant work experience in at least one other industry? Should they be expected to think through potential disruption of and actively participate in disrupting the core business as part of an assignment through strategy and innovation functions? Should they be asked to gain experience building a new division or a new competency earlier on in their careers? Should they have failed at something at least once before they are considered to be future leaders?

Every company needs to determine the right leadership formula, and there is no "one size fits all." One top five biopharmaceutical company experimented several years ago in bringing in an industry outsider, placing a bet that new thinking unencumbered by a lifetime spent in the industry would spark innovation. This experiment did not deliver the desired outcome, and the outsider was replaced by a long-term insider who returned to a so-far proven formula of mergers, portfolio rationalization, and cost-cutting which investors and the financial community have seemed to reward. Whether this experience reflects limitations on the experience profile, individual competency, or fit is not clear, but we expect to see similar experiments with increasing frequency as traditional distinctions between sectors in healthcare break down.

TRADITIONAL LEADERS   **NEW LEADERS**

New leadership model.

We are not alone in this view on the relationship between leadership competencies and success in innovating. Virtually every leader we interviewed from across the healthcare ecosystem attributed a good part of success—their own and their organizations'—to having a clear and consistently articulated vision for what innovation means to them and their organization. William Fleming from Humana confirmed the importance of having an articulated, communicated, and continually re-enforced vision for the future. At Humana, the focus is on increasing Healthy Days for its members. He also spoke about his reflections on the "shadow he casts" as a leader regarding personal attitudes on the topic of innovation and accompanying behaviors displayed for the entire organization to observe which must go far beyond what is formally stated in company/department mission statements.

Blasine Penkowski of J&J has seen the importance and value of leadership starting with the CEO in creating an internal climate free of cynicism as it relates to the importance of innovation as an element of the core culture. She believes that innovation cannot be considered someone's pet project but must permeate the entire organization. However, this process can be accelerated by creating pockets of innovation, protecting them, and then highlighting achievements as a source of organizational pride.

Michael Dowling, CEO of Northwell Health is a firm believer of "anything is possible as long as the right people are on the team." In his view, an articulated vision consistently demonstrated by all levels of leadership is essential to stimulate innovative, transformational thinking. He also believes that achieving the desired level of change can sometimes only be realized by deliberately bringing in new leaders from outside who share a vision for the future. He observed that "sometimes it is easier to change (i.e., replace) people than to change people," reflecting on a willingness to make the tough decisions needed to stay ahead of a rapidly evolving market.

Alain Serhan from Egon Zehnder discussed a different slant on leadership as reflected in the research his organization is carrying out in collaboration with Harvard professor Linda Hill. In their view, the pace of change in the external environment is more complex and is occurring so rapidly that the top leader should no longer be expected to be THE one defining the vision that the organization needs to understand and embrace. If that vision happens to be the "right one," by the time everyone is onboard, the original vision is most likely already obsolete. In this new approach, the critical success factor is focused on creating the context that enables innovation and agility throughout the organization. The role of the leader is still crucial, but it is less about pointing the way and more about setting expectations, nurturing a trusting, collaborative environment—one that favors individual and organizational agile learning and one that facilitates decision-making. Years of executives' assessment data from Egon Zehnder have shown that generally, leaders develop one style and rarely vary it. To create this innovation-friendly context, leaders need to master an ability to vary the style of management, of influence, of decision-making, which is a very different approach that may challenge even progressive leaders who have grown up in the highly regulated and relatively slow pace that the pharma industry has worked in until quite recently. For example, a critical success factor in their opinion has to do with managing conflict. Typically, in most organizations conflict is something that is discouraged and "managed," i.e., get rid of it and the people who are associated with triggering it. In a world that is changing rapidly, the role of the leader may instead be to encourage "managed conflict" as a way of generating transformational ideas. Once a leader has nurtured a trusting environment that allows for creative conflicts, his/her style needs to pivot to encourage the organization's decision-making abilities to harvest the value of the managed conflict. Some refer to demonstrating these attributes as *adaptive* or *contextual* leadership.

Amy Edmondson, Professor at Harvard Business School, has observed success from leaders who exhibit three sets of behaviors—setting the stage and framing the work for others; creating the right climate for innovation, which requires having the confidence to acknowledge when they don't have all of the answers; and promoting learning from failures rather than penalizing attempts to do different things or to do things differently.

This spectrum of views confirms the opportunity for every organization to find the leadership style that is fit for purpose for a time and place along its corporate development journey. However, it also confirms that there is no task more important than finding and grooming leaders that can think about today and tomorrow congruently. Are these the aptitudes and competencies required of biopharma leaders? Should the premium that is placed on industry experience be replaced by seeking outsiders who aren't experts on "how biopharma works" to challenge inherent assumptions and drive the next stage of growth for the industry?

Teaming the Right Talent

> "Great things in business are never done by one person. They're done by a team of people."
>
> **Steve Jobs**

In the world of premier management consulting firms, finding high-performing project teams is typically the norm. The problem to be solved defines the project approach, project teams, and duration. Consulting companies are in the business of advisory talent, and hire and train their employees to be analytical problem-solvers first, subject matter experts next. It is therefore typically easy to build teams from their ranks based on project needs. Successful project performance determines the future career trajectory of team members and establishes the path to their professional growth. At the same time, the cost of failure is high. For the employees, it is typically an up or out scenario, and for the consulting company, it either gains a repeat customer or loses future business.

Across various industry sectors and particularly within the biopharmaceutical industry, finding the right talent and building strong innovation teams from within the internal talent pool is a much more complicated process. Internal talent tends to be subject matter- and management-focused first. The path to career progress is relatively linear, at least to certain seniority levels. The focus on documented functional expertise creates a situation in which there are often limited opportunities for some of the most innovative individuals in the organization to take on various cross-functional roles. The opportunities to work in a matrixed environment where they can broaden their cross-functional understanding of the workings of the industry and their own skill sets are also limited. Furthermore, the optimal size of teams in traditional functions (marketing, sales, medical, HR, legal, etc.) can be easily benchmarked and staffed as they are the core drivers of the business. Building optimal teams for functions such as strategy and innovation tends to be more difficult as they are not near-term revenue-generating functions. A lot of strategic thinking is outsourced to consultants. Long-term strategic planning focuses on sustaining the core business, and investments are seldom made in disruptive innovation. For many internal strategy and innovation team members, career development opportunities tend to be limited. The strategy & innovation function that should be thinking hard about future evolution and sustenance of companies often tends to be resource- and investment-constrained; and at times it is merely a project management office to interact with and guide outside consultants.

Identifying the strongest internal employees and recruiting the right talent from outside the organization to meet specific strategy, innovation, or transformation needs that may evolve across a company's business cycle is one of the most critical tasks of any leader. When examined in the context of creating and driving a balanced innovation portfolio and culture, it can be definitive in predicting future success.

As discussed before, within the incumbents of the biopharmaceutical industry product-focused innovation is regarded to be the primary domain of the R&D function. However, in thinking about how to launch and integrate a broader innovation agenda, the incumbents should look to other industries for which the business transformation cycle is typically shorter due to the absence of inherent technological barriers in the form of patents and market exclusivity. Such an examination might suggest the opportunity to organize the innovation function outside of R&D. Fast-moving consumer goods and consumer-oriented technology solutions come to mind. From within the industry, the evolution and integration of the Health Economics and Outcomes Research (HEOR) groups that now exist in virtually every biopharmaceutical company provide an excellent blueprint for building internal innovation departments. When it started to become clear that the cost of biopharmaceuticals would be increasingly challenged and that market access rather than regulatory approval would be the primary predictor of success, companies began to look for new skill sets and enablers in the form of HEOR professionals. Initially, the focus of newly created HEOR departments was on systematically determining the burden of illness regarding the impact on the individual and populations, as well as economic costs. Then efforts were made to quantify and model the budget impact of the new product but also the cost offsets in, for example, hospitalization avoidance or sparing other medical resource utilization. More recently companies are generating real-world evidence on how new therapies perform outside the RCT environment that can inform outcomes-based contracts to link reimbursement with real-world performance. What began as a "nice to have" small group recruited from academia has now evolved to a fully integrated and critical strategic function in determining which products enter development, how they are developed, and increasingly how they drive the commercialization process as payers versus providers become the definitive customer segment. One can speculate as to whether companies that successfully launch and cultivate innovation groups will derive similar benefits and competitive advantage.

In our view, within the biopharmaceutical industry, the internal innovation teams should have the same seat at the table as the core functions such as R&D, medicine, marketing, or sales. Built over time, they would understand the DNA of the parent organization, its appetite for change, and focus on both sustaining the core business and searching for the new. We discuss the pros and cons of having internal innovation teams focused on core, adjacent, and breakthrough innovations in the chapter on Developing New Ventures. Whether setting up innovation units up for the first time or managing their development over time, the critical leadership tasks include assembling the right talent and skill sets, developing a strong team spirit, and providing clear opportunities for growth to these team members. A simple reality check would be to ensure that individual performance objectives and associated incentive payments mandate a time allocation for work outside the core business.

Talent Mix

Based on our experience, it takes six fundamental role types to form a strong innovation team (Figure 7.1):

Innovation Leader: Finding people to take on the roles of leaders of innovation in the biopharmaceutical industry is not easy. These individuals need to have an understanding of the healthcare ecosystem and roles individual stakeholders play; they should be able to articulate a clear vision; should be well steeped in the innovation process; and should have product development

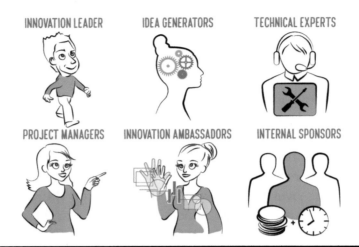

Figure 7.1 Teaming the right talent/six critical roles.

and launch experience, strong influencing skills and a strong management skillset. Most importantly, they must have a passion for succeeding and the courage to fail. Along with the executive sponsor described later, the Innovation Leader must also be an active adopter and proponent of the 80-80 Rule to ensure that speed in project selection and an appropriate and challenging level of risk tolerance help shape and guide the innovation agenda for the organization.

Idea Generators: Idea Generators cannot be identified by looking at levels on an organizational chart as they may exist in all areas of the organization. Companies need to create opportunities for such talent to self-identify via techniques such as innovation forums, internal contests/crowd-sourcing, and allocating a defined percentage of performance objectives to non-core activities. Leadership must then help these people harness and further develop their interests via cross-functional projects to avoid frustration.

Technical Experts: Technical Experts, as the name suggests, are skilled at translating ideas into practical, contextual products or solutions that can be brought to the market. They are typically characterized as individuals with deep functional experience (e.g., regulatory, pharmacovigilance, procurement, legal, compliance, IT, etc.) and a strong track-record of performance and internal credibility. Initially, they may appear to be potential roadblocks to innovation as they may see their primary role as limiting risk for the organization. However, once they understand the critical nature of experimentation for future success and how risk-taking can be "smart" if applied correctly within appropriate guard rails and governance, they can become productive proponents of the 80-80 Rule and change agents themselves.

Project Managers: Project Managers are critical to managing the development and execution of new products and services in the market. While project management skills are valuable across the board in almost all roles in today's matrixed work environments, there is value in having a dedicated group who is recognized within the organization and empowered to provide structure, establish and manage a governance model with defined decision criteria and pathways, and drive resource allocation.

Innovation Ambassadors: Generally found in the ranks of middle management, Innovation Ambassadors can play a critical role in driving internal alignment. They are typically well known and well connected within the organization, are entirely open to embracing and supporting new ideas, and are excited (not scared or pessimistic) by the uncertainty and the opportunity to contribute beyond their formal areas of responsibility.

Strong Internal Sponsors: Ideally this should be the CEO but can be delegated one level down if the selected individual possesses the necessary level of internal (and ideally external) credibility to stand on their own. In addition, this role could be a significant training ground for the CEO-in-waiting.

Organizational structures themselves don't guarantee success but can be a crucial enabler if set up correctly, or a source of significant inertia and back-sliding if not. We will elaborate on the pros and cons of various organizational structures when we discuss principles relative to Developing New Ventures.

We have discussed before that it can be challenging to find disrupters and change agents from within the industry since most people have grown up in the business accepting the widespread beliefs about biopharma-unique critical success factors. Historically, such attempts have mostly resulted in a low level of differentiation in the commercial model and customer engagement approach since most people are experts within a narrowly defined set of expertise parameters. Furthermore, there is a bias against bringing in people from outside the industry. One often hears sentiments expressed such as "They just don't understand how pharma works" and "They won't be able to get anything done in such a highly regulated industry." This institutionalized bias contributes to the continued perpetuation of a universal and undifferentiated business model and can be one of the most significant barriers to innovation.

Adopting the tenets of the 80-80 Rule and applying them as a fundamental component of an incumbent organizations' talent acquisition strategy is critical. Bringing in people from other industries to challenge the status quo and expand the range of the possible may be one of the most vital elements of building an innovation program. To be sure, such individuals will need to be carefully mentored and partnered with creative and open-minded people from within the company who do have the necessary understanding of the real (versus perceived) boundaries and barriers. These individuals can help the external visionaries translate their ideas into a language that can be understood and embraced by the broader organization.

Joseph La Barge from Spark Therapeutics shared with us that while they don't have a specific employee profile for hiring decisions, they tend to bring into the organization people with diverse backgrounds who are curious and collaborative. They are attracted to innovating, figuring things out for the first time, and dedicated to putting the patient first. He describes their corporate culture as being based on a goal that employees "don't follow footsteps, but instead create the path" and contrasts that with what occurs in most large biopharma companies that may inhibit the rate at which they can innovate.

Amy Edmondson attributes the failure of many outsiders to the fact that companies often have not performed a specific gap analysis to identify missing capabilities, which should drive the search for talent from outside. Or sometimes, when they have conducted a gap analysis, it may not have been done transparently enough, to allow the results to be openly shared across the organization. As a result, people inside the organization may not be set up to help those brought in from outside to be successful; insider's willingness to support outsiders' success requires that insiders don't see the outsiders as either a de facto criticism of insiders or as a threat. In such circumstances organizations need to be good at bridging cultural differences between internal and external talent and mount efforts that could be characterized as "extreme teaming."

Reflections on the Experiment in Challenging the Status Quo

At Boehringer Ingelheim, it was the initial success of several experiments in new business opportunities and ways of working and engaging with customers that provided us the impetus to embark on a more formal examination of innovation. Other companies may choose to begin with a more formal process to define the innovation agenda. In either case, essential elements should include:

- Ensuring the focus on innovation and new ways of working are included in the overarching corporate vision, annual company-wide goals, and associated incentives, so employees are clear they have "permission" to innovate;

- Taking the opportunity to position new initiatives within a formal innovation framework to make it clear to everyone whether they are intended to support the core business, test adjacencies, or identify a potential pathway towards a new business;
- Aligning incentives and securing buy-in upfront from the various groups that will be needed to fund, design, and deliver the initiatives;
- Pro-actively examining standard operating procedures and elements of the existing culture and "the way we do things around here" so that they do not get in the way of progress when plowing new ground;
- More formally diagnosing and addressing gaps in new competencies for leaders and other employees within the company that will be required to innovate;
- Granting organizational permission to challenge and create an expectation of accountability for constructively stimulating and managing conflict; and
- Carrying out joint innovation readiness assessments with external partner organizations to anticipate as many potential roadblocks as possible.

In the end, it is the combination of a consistent, enlightened leadership; the right investment for a sustained duration; the right talent mix; the right team spirit; the right culture; courage; and some luck that will determine the success or failure of an innovation enterprise. Incumbents, as well as new entrants should embrace this thinking as they look to set up for exploring new frontiers.

Endnote

1. Bansi Nagji and Geoff Tuff, "Managing Your Innovation Portfolio," *Harvard Business Review*, May 2012.

Chapter 8

Finding White Spaces

"I was seldom able to see an opportunity until it had ceased to be one."

Mark Twain

There are different ways to think about white spaces in the context of business strategy. A few typical examples range from finding markets with no or limited competition, finding gaps in existing markets or product lines, or creating entirely new products or businesses. We introduced "Smart integrated Medicine" and an associated commercial model as a potential white space for biopharmaceutical industry to capture. Similarly, businesses can look for white spaces internally by examining the current portfolio and capabilities versus need to grow the current business, or externally with a view toward the opportunities created by evolving markets. We have summarized these dimensions and the associated impact on funding innovation into a principle: "Embrace the Need, Money Will Follow."

Furthermore, innovation efforts identified through the lens of organization-specific strategic interests and capabilities without a clear alignment with external white spaces that have the highest potential for return will often lead to value destruction, not value creation. Similar to a traditional product-focused research approach in the biopharmaceutical industry, disciplined efforts to finding external white spaces and prioritizing innovation efforts that go beyond the current portfolio, internal company capabilities, and even conventional industry boundaries are critical. We call this principle: "Outside In First, Inside Out Next."

The pragmatic approach is to consider the above two principles together as organizations embark on the journey of finding, evaluating, and capitalizing on white spaces. The previously discussed innovation framework categorized innovation initiatives as core, adjacent, or breakthrough. While core initiatives may align best with organization-specific interests and capabilities, adjacent and breakthrough initiatives by definition focus on external white spaces (Figure 8.1). As discussed previously, leadership needs to enable a well-balanced innovation portfolio across the range of core, adjacent, and breakthrough initiatives in a mix that fits each company's strategic intent and risk tolerance. Challenging the organization to think about white spaces beyond the core business but within a framework that is aligned with the overall strategy will enable appropriate funding and allocation of human capital toward white-space initiatives.

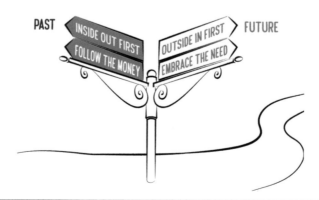

Figure 8.1   Finding white spaces requires following a new path.

Embrace the Need, Money Will Follow

"Chase the vision, not the money; the money will
end up following you."

Tony Hsieh, CEO of Zappos

The suggestion that one should "Follow the Money" was
popularized in "All the President's Men," a film portraying the
Watergate scandal of the 1970s. But in our view, the more
appropriate thing to say as it relates to funding innovation is
"Embrace the need, money will follow."

Western society and capitalism are built on the notion
of consumption. In fact, this has been the driver of most
of the innovation and associated economic growth our
world has seen since the industrial revolution. And if one
looks at the innovations that spawned new industries and
generated financial windfalls, they often, either consciously or
unconsciously, solved for unmet needs or in many cases needs
we didn't even realize existed.

Development of steam-powered locomotives is an
excellent example of "following the need" that led to "money
following." Historically speaking, Hero of Alexandria is
credited with creating the aeolipile—the first steam engine
that demonstrated the power of steam to drive propulsion.
However, it was not until the early seventeenth century that
the steam-powered engines started to be used to replace brute
manpower and horsepower, with its first application in mining
operations. As coal mines got deeper, there was a more urgent
need to pump out the groundwater found in these mines.
Jerónimo de Ayanz in 1606, followed by Thomas Savery in
1705 and then Thomas Newcomen in 1711, built steam engines
that not only greatly improved mining operations, but also
started to find adjacent use in pumping water required for
industrial manufacturing. The first breakthrough application of
the steam engine technology happened in 1765 when James
Watt created a vastly improved and efficient steam engine that

would not only find application in mining, but also power the automation of manufacturing in the factories during the industrial revolution. It is also an example of "following the need," where steam engine technology was applied to the unmet need for vast amounts of power required in industrial manufacturing and ultimately led to the economic renaissance in western Europe.

Then, in 1814, George Stephenson developed the steam-powered locomotive to solve for the unmet need to carry coal economically over long distances. Applied to the problem of public transportation, the steam locomotive created an entirely new mode of transport and industry. Over time, it led to a significant capital windfall for not only the railroad companies but also many adjacent sectors, such as finance and steel. Cornelius Vanderbilt, J.P. Morgan, and Andrew Carnegie are a few of the industrial stalwarts that rose to prominence (also known as robber barons for the sometimes unethical business practices employed to grow their business empires). Vanderbilt built a railroad empire, Carnegie supplied steel required to build railroads and bridges, and Morgan financed it. The British empire in part owes the expansion of its colonial powers in India and Africa to the vast rail networks it laid there to streamline the movement of raw materials on the back of financing driven by local taxes and tariffs. If George Stephenson had focused on "following the money" which at that time was in mining and industrial manufacturing, and not thought of applying the technology to transportation to consciously fulfill an unmet need, we would have never created the global railway or steel industries.

As a more recent example, the mobile phone initially had one purpose—an innovative device that enabled communications from anywhere, anytime. Just when people realized the power of the Internet to find information, communicate, and engage in commerce, the smartphone took this power a quantum leap forward by simultaneously making the functionality entirely portable, less expensive, and at speeds much faster than previously possible at the same time. Such portability has ended up disrupting big industries such as transportation (Uber, Waymo), retail (Amazon, Alibaba), and even healthcare (virtual visits such as Doctor on Demand, Teladoc).

Until recently, in most major U.S. cities, the local Taxi and Limousine authority held a virtual monopoly on pricing and the associated customer experience (for better or worse) and determined (and in most cases limited) who could be a driver via a tightly controlled permit/medallion system. Uber and more recently competitors such as Lyft leveraged smartphone capabilities coupled with a much more flexible and open driver-participation model to turn the taxi industry upside down. Companies like Uber and Lyft are a brilliant example of not only embracing the need for better availability and pricing of local transportation, but also helping to completely redefine the need from merely providing transportation to redesigning all aspects of the customer experience associated with such transportation.

A similar trend can be observed in the history and development of the modern biotechnology industry. There are several working definitions of biotechnology, but all fundamentally incorporate the idea of harnessing living systems and organisms to develop or make products. Humankind has employed living organisms in agriculture for thousands of years via selective breeding and hybridization of plants and animals. Most of us are well acquainted with the application of fermentation to produce alcoholic beverages. In the early twentieth century, biotechnology principles were directed toward manufacturing corn starch to produce acetone for explosives used in WWI and a more positive application in the production of antibiotics. The field of modern biotechnology as it relates to medicine is associated with experiments from the early 1970s in gene splicing and transferring mammalian genetic material coding for proteins and antibodies into simpler organisms that could then be grown in culture to produce substances of interest. As emerging medical understanding about the underlying causes of disease converged with the development of technology (synthetic chemistry, recombinant DNA, cell culture), it became possible to treat, and in some cases cure, a much broader range of conditions. If biopharmaceutical companies at the time had looked at these developments purely as interesting academic findings and continued to "follow the money" available for treating chronic diseases with small molecule therapeutics, one can only speculate where the industry and medicine would be today. Instead, visionary leaders and financiers were willing to allocate and apply resources for more than ten years until the FDA approval of the first diagnostics and therapeutics derived from biotechnology in the mid-1980s. Development of biotechnology-based medicines was a clear example of embracing the need associated with complex and challenging-to-treat conditions and diseases and innovating within white spaces from both external market and internal capabilities perspectives.

While the most dramatic examples of finding and capitalizing on white spaces often involve technological breakthroughs as in steam engines, mobile phones, and biotechnology, there are examples where either development or marketing strategy has led to finding new applications of existing technology. Viagra and Flomax are two examples from the biopharma industry that created what is known today as the "lifestyle drugs" market—a new category in the industry filling an unmet need not recognized before.

It is well known that Pfizer's Viagra was initially under development for several cardio-vascular indications including as an anti-hypertensive. While the blood-pressure-lowering properties were judged to be modest, attentive researchers identified an effect that could be considered as unwanted in the original context but a significant attribute in the context of erectile dysfunction. The resulting pharmaceutical from a "failed" research program coupled with education and Direct-to-Consumer (DTC) advertising campaigns created a completely new "lifestyle disease" category within which Viagra became a blockbuster product.

Boehringer Ingelheim leveraged a creative marketing approach for the Direct-to-Consumer (DTC) advertising campaign for Flomax. It introduced the "BPH Boys" who, with a tinge of humor, educated men that frequent urination caused by Benign Prostatic Hyperplasia (BPH) could be viewed as a "badge of honor" for membership in the middle-aged men's club of sports enthusiasts. They also positioned BPH as a lifestyle condition relatively easy to self-diagnose and very treatable without surgery. In addition to fulfilling a previously unmet clinical need, providing a valuable educational service, and generating solid financial returns, treating BPH with Flomax became part of the popular culture during the mid-2000s, referenced in films and by celebrities on late-night talk shows.

The Viagra and Flomax examples illustrate the creation of an entirely new, multi-billion-dollar market focused on a new category of so-called lifestyle conditions, which have continued to accrue increased credibility and economic returns with aging baby boomers. Initially used for treating disorders related to muscle spasms, Botox as a cosmetic treatment of forehead lines, crow's feet lines, and glabellar lines has created economic windfalls for Allergan. Lately, there is an effort to recognize obesity as a chronic condition. Such recognition would allow the healthcare ecosystem, from providers to biopharmaceutical companies, to be reimbursed for managing obesity. One could speculate that new guidelines regarding acceptable blood-sugar or blood-pressure levels create new white spaces for development and marketing of healthcare products and services.

Not all these innovations were deliberate solutions for an identified unmet need. Many were trying to solve for one thing but accidentally solved for another. At times, technological developments enabled the pursuit of other, more significant, unidentified, unmet needs, created a new customer experience and in some cases entirely new markets, based on attributes that we didn't realize we needed.

Despite these well-known examples, one can't always hope to serendipitously recognize unmet needs or identify needs that we are not aware of. As the white spaces in traditional biopharmaceutical products continue to shrink, biopharmaceutical companies need to broaden their aperture as they look for new opportunities. A structured approach is required to stay on this course; one that is focused on solving for the known unmet need but allows room for accidental discovery of not-yet-identified white space opportunities that can spawn new businesses and economies. The application of the 80-80 Rule in this situation is critical for both the innovator and the investor. The innovator must be prepared to identify and support parallel opportunities that lie outside the defined targets in strategic plans; in effect, the structured approach must be paradoxically grounded in the unstructured ability to see what is not apparent to everyone else. Similarly, the investor must be willing to shift the allocation of at least some portion of resources to quickly investigate the economic potential of what might otherwise be viewed as tangential or worse a "failure" relative to the original plans. Lastly, sustained level of investment over time is critical for initiatives to yield results.

Outside In First, Inside Out Next

> "No problem can be solved by the same consciousness that created it. We need to see the world anew."
>
> **Albert Einstein**

The fallacy of incumbent businesses is that they tend to think inside out first versus outside in. Being successful at the core for such a long time, they keep trying to find ways to sustain their core business even as markets shift. Incumbent R&D functions tend to double down on what they have done best in the past, and seldom broaden their aperture to look for opportunities beyond narrowly defined markets that the business starts to operate in as it matures. As a result, they often fail to read what the market might be telling them—the need to cannibalize themselves or get cannibalized. There are multiple examples: East India Company, Kodak, and Blockbuster, to name a few. And many other industries today are watching with fear: car rental agencies due to Uber, Uber due to driverless cars, every known industry due to Amazon.

The biopharmaceutical industry often seems to behave as if it is immune to this phenomenon of rapid disruption, especially when it comes to its core offering—the molecule-based biopharmaceutical product. Is the pharmaceutical industry right in believing this trend of historical success can continue?

No one has the crystal ball. But we would advocate that all incumbents, including biopharmaceutical companies, should set up formal mechanisms that, with a sense of urgency bordering on paranoia, scan the external, global environment for anything and everything that might disrupt and ultimately cannibalize their current business. In fact, given that patients are more and more willing to experiment with different sites of care that go beyond the traditional physician's office or the hospital, including Urgent Care centers and telemedicine, we think there are immense white space opportunities that are presenting themselves for biopharmaceutical companies to find new sources of value.

As it relates to the core, the biopharmaceutical industry's Business Development teams are geared to look outside to academia and venture-backed start-ups for new molecules or enabling technologies and then acquiring the Intellectual Property rights to do what it does best—clinical development, steering the resultant products through the regulatory process, and commercialization. The 80-80 Rule comes into play significantly in biopharma business development activities. The same externally directed approach needs to be embraced as it relates to allied technology and solutions that can be molded into adjacent or breakthrough innovation opportunities given the changing market landscape.

Often, even as it relates to the core, many companies struggle with the "not invented here syndrome" where external opportunities don't compete well with products from internal research since it is always possible to ask for more data on which to base decisions. This dilemma becomes even more relevant when dealing with start-ups that may give rise to adjacent or breakthrough opportunities as they are geared to taking risks and fast prototyping which may just not fit with typical biopharma culture. By investing in and building up capabilities grounded in an outside-in perspective coupled with a structured approach to identifying relevant white spaces as discussed earlier, incumbents will discover options that can be leveraged in the near term to strengthen their core business or spawn adjacent businesses. They might also find the unicorns that could be the next businesses the incumbents become.

Capturing White Spaces in COPD Treatment: A Case Study

With an appropriate hypothesis and adequate investment in place, several steps can be followed to enable a structured process of further evaluating and capturing white spaces. Let us illustrate these steps through an example of work in applying smart technology as an adjacent innovation to the inhaler-based Chronic Obstructive Pulmonary Disease (COPD) medications developed and marketed by several industry incumbents including Boehringer Ingelheim, GSK, and Novartis.

As a first step, market assessments in combination with internal experience with the markets can help organizations identify the dimensions along which a product, technology, or solution is likely to progress and most likely fulfill identified customer needs. For example, current players all seem to have examined the challenges and opportunities of respiratory medication delivery and are focused on factors related to improving adherence and advancing the quality of communication between patients and providers regarding treatment.

The second step is to identify the position the organization occupies along the identified dimensions relative to competition and internal capabilities, and where it can differentiate and succeed. For example, the RESPIMAT device is Boehringer Ingelheim's platform technology for delivering inhaled medications via a unique soft mist. The company's strong position in the respiratory market represented an advantage on which to build additional functionality for the RESPIMAT device.

The third step is to identify the best approach to activate the new features and functionality in the market. In the Boehringer Ingelheim example, the third step involved an acknowledgement that external collaborations could provide an opportunity for product enhancement via the application of digital technology to complement the RESPIMAT device. Novartis and GSK took a similar approach. Propeller Health and QUALCOMM were identified as external organizations that specialize in technology and analytics related to customizing Bluetooth-enabled devices that track the timing of inhaler actuation and recording related events and environmental factors determined to be relevant to treatment. Co-development partnerships were formed, with the objective as viewed by Boehringer Ingelheim "to create some of the real-world market experience of technology so the providers will be willing to provide it, the patients will be willing to adopt a sensor and basically drive adherence."[1]

This effort is a clear example of evolving these companies' strategic mandate from "this is what we do as an organization" to "this is where our market is or should be heading." The companies have "embraced the need" for better COPD management through adherence assistance and enhanced patient-provider dialog. They looked "Outside In First," to identify the white space and find partners that could assist with developing the solutions that could help it capture the white space opportunity in COPD management.

More recently, Express Scripts, one of the largest Pharmacy Benefit Managers in the United States, has signed a deal with Propeller Health. According to the press release, "the idea behind the program is to help patients avoid over-using their so-called 'rescue inhalers,' which could worsen symptoms over time, and to make sure they don't neglect their controller medications that can be taken at any time to prevent flare-ups. Essentially, it's about saving money by helping patients prevent bad and expensive outcomes, like trips to the emergency room."[2] While for biopharmaceutical companies such as GSK, Novartis, and Boehringer Ingelheim, partnerships with start-ups such as Propeller Health and others have focused on increasing medication adherence to help patients manage COPD and reduce overall healthcare costs, they have also seen the associated potential uptick in volume as an economic benefit. Express Scripts is looking at such a partnership to lower the total cost of care for COPD patients. Both stakeholders in the industry ecosystem recognize the same white space. Now the question is: Who will be able to capture the economic benefit associated with healthcare cost containment—the biopharma industry or the pharmacy benefit manager?

We see the 80-80 Rule at work here. Waiting for certainty and minimizing risk before moving ahead with all of the examples offered in this section would almost certainly mean that another incumbent organization or even a previously unrecognized competitor will get there ahead of you. In the current healthcare ecosystem, the traditional balance of power between various industry stakeholders is being disrupted, and everyone is competing to capture the available dollars in the market. Those who embrace the 80-80 Rule and the principles of rapid experimentation in the market will capture the new value opportunities better than those who try to perfect solutions. This approach is a significant shift from the traditional biopharmaceutical development model—and requires a fundamental change in approach to developing new ventures that go beyond the molecule.

Endnotes

1. John Comstock, "Propeller, Boehringer Ingelheim Expand into Broad Commercial Partnership," *mobihealthnews*, March 23, 2016, accessed January 20, 2018, http://www.mobihealthnews.com/content/propeller-boehringer-ingelheim-expand-broad-commercial-partnership
2. Christina Farr, "Express Scripts Signs a Deal with Start-up Propeller Health as It Ups Investment in Digital Health," *CNBC.com*, November 15, 2017, accessed January 20, 2018, https://www.cnbc.com/2017/11/15/express-scripts-partners-with-propeller-health.html

Chapter 9

Developing New Ventures

"I skate to where the puck is going to be, not where it has been."

—Wayne Gretzky, ice hockey great

The biopharmaceutical industry has deep expertise in developing products within the confines of a highly regulated and defined process. In fact, historically its product development capabilities have been a source of competitive advantage. However, developing new ventures in the adjacent and breakthrough spaces requires a different mindset. It requires a willingness to look beyond past bases of success when scanning the horizon for new opportunities and embracing risk, as we advocate, through the principles of the 80-80 Rule.

First, there is the question of organizational facilitation of new ventures. As we have noted before, teaming the right talent and building strong innovation teams focused on a balanced portfolio of core, adjacent, and breakthrough innovation is one of the critical determinants of success. However, even with the right innovation intent in place, developing new adjacent and breakthrough ventures within the organizational context of the core business can sometimes be difficult. One, despite an explicit allocation of investment dollars, there will always be pressure to reallocate money from new ventures to core business given the short-term profitability targets. In such cases, the core will typically win, and without sustained investment over time, new initiatives will mostly languish. Two, by setting up an innovation team within the organizational construct of the core business, the leadership may send a subtle yet unintended message that core teams are not focused on innovation or innovative practices. This unintentional consequence creates another barrier to the development of new ventures. Three, unique to the biopharmaceutical industry, the legal and compliance framework that is required to operate the core business limits the flexibility necessary to develop and test new ventures within the standard operating procedures of the core organization and often causes delays. Lastly, new ventures could sometimes be a threat to the current business of one's customers, or negatively impact the relationships with existing customers as they may see these initiatives as disruptors to their existing business.

Innovation work focused on the core business needs to happen within the core organization. However, work focused on new ventures—either adjacent or breakthrough, given the reasons above—is ideally conducted under an organizational construct separate from the core business. In such cases, it should have an independent structure, governance, funding, processes, and metrics. At the same time, there should be flexibility to leverage the core capabilities of the parent organization that may be required to develop the new ventures. This flexibility may come in the form of job rotations for select individuals or other methods of resource sharing. Lastly, one should also consider how the core organizational capabilities may be leveraged to scale up new adjacent and breakthrough ventures as they mature and are ready for commercialization.

For example, Renault-Nissan-Mitsubishi Alliance CEO Carlos Ghosn plans to start a $1 billion corporate venture capital fund to invest in start-ups developing technologies such as vehicle electrification, autonomous systems, connectivity, and artificial intelligence. The group will be set up as a separate legal entity with independent processes for working nimbly and quickly with far smaller start-ups. Within the biopharmaceutical industry, the team at Otsuka that has successfully launched the Digital Medicine System: Abilify MyCite® (aripiprazole tablets with Proteus sensor) was set up as a new venture team firewalled from the core Otsuka business. One could contemplate that such a setup allowed the team to work rapidly without competing with the daily priorities and standard operating procedures of the core business. At the same time, this team was able to leverage the core competencies of a biopharmaceutical company in obtaining regulatory approval for biopharmaceutical products to do the same for the digital medicine system.

While there is no right or wrong answer, every organization and its leadership needs to define the best structure within their organizational context to ensure sustained facilitation of innovation efforts. For new entrants, on the other hand, building flexibility early on for future adjacent and breakthrough efforts should become a fundamental organizational design principle.

Beyond the organizational context, we propose three additional principles that should guide new ventures development:

Design for the End User, but Consider the Ecosystem

Having a clear target customer or market segment should drive all development activities. However, it is also essential to simulate the impact of new ventures across the entire ecosystem to identify and leverage critical enablers and identify and remove barriers to success for investment in the pre-launch phase.

I (Ruchin) trained as an architect. As part of that training, we learned about design thinking and system-level thinking and applying them simultaneously in every situation. Design thinking focuses on creating the best user experience based on feedback from the user (in this case, the end product was a building—a house, a hotel, an airport). On the other hand, system-level thinking focuses on how the product will interact with the environment it will sit in (in this case, the house next door, the road in the front, the connection to utilities, etc.). Being able to design a product or service from the end user perspective makes it better for the user—but also developing it from the standpoint of how it will interplay in, and become a seamless part of, the broader ecosystem is critical to market adoption and commercialization. Considering the entire ecosystem rather than focusing only on pre-defined end-user requirements is also more likely to uncover unmet or underappreciated needs and new opportunities as we have discussed in the section devoted to working in white spaces.

Keep It Modular

Another concept that comes in handy when developing new ventures is the concept of modularity. There is modularity all around us. Consider the USB stick: It serves a simple purpose of data storage and transfer between various data and visualization platforms. It can store multiple kinds of data—text, images, voice, movies—and plug into a vast host of devices used in everyday settings—computers, phones, television, A/V receivers, tablets. You can plug it into machines at work and now even in your car. All it needs is a receptacle.

Doors and windows are designed to fit standard openings in building construction. Locksets manufactured by different manufacturers can fit the doors and windows from any manufacturer. Faucets are designed to fit in bathroom or kitchen sinks produced by various manufacturers. Modular doesn't get simpler than this. It is akin to the concept of interoperability in the technology industry. Some would say that the pharmaceutical pill is very modular. You take it out of its package and ingest it. Digital therapeutics incorporate inherent modular properties. They can be developed to complement a specific biopharmaceutical product, function across an entire therapeutic category, or exert their effect independent of any conventional product. Modularity, if applied to healthcare, can solve for rapid adoption of new ventures in the highly complex healthcare ecosystem.

Keep It Simple

Health is one of the simplest experiences we have as human beings—either we feel healthy, or we don't. While health itself is simple, healthcare is complex. Our need as individuals is straightforward (to feel healthy), but when interacting with the healthcare ecosystem, we are suddenly surrounded by a complex web of treatment choices, delivery mechanisms, and payments. The burden of dealing with all of this, one can argue, adds to the difficulty of feeling sick. This imbalance between the simple need for health and the complex healthcare ecosystem built to deliver health is one of the most significant paradoxes of our times. We call it the "simplicity deficit" in healthcare.

I (Ruchin) had the opportunity to visit a few hospitals in China. What caught my eye was that at every point of interaction between the patient and the hospital, whether it was check-in or picking up a prescription, there was a screen with a green, a yellow and a red smiley face (Figure 9.1). It gave a straightforward option for the patient to provide feedback on the service received. Imagine the effect

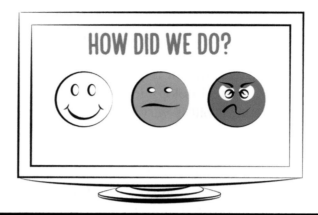

Figure 9.1   Real-time customer feedback.

on the healthcare system if it were feasible to receive and
respond to end-to-end feedback across the ecosystem and
strive for more greens than reds? How about we think of
every new healthcare innovation from the perspective of
simplicity of interaction? And how about we aim to transform
every current healthcare interaction to be as simple as
possible?

Historically, the biopharmaceutical industry has done
simple well. For most primary care diseases, one could directly
manage the symptoms of the disease by ingesting a pill. Even
for complex specialty diseases, the effort has been to simplify
the delivery mechanism—whether oral, transdermal, or
infused. While the science behind the pill is highly complex,
the industry has successfully delivered on simple consumption
mechanisms for the end users.

Given the historical strengths of the three core design
principles for new ventures, the biopharmaceutical industry
may be uniquely positioned to serve as an integrator across
the healthcare ecosystem. In the current biopharma model
where the product is the core value proposition, it is left to
the customer to understand where the product fits and how
benefits are derived. Customer groups have historically been
defined and treated as discrete entities given the complex

range of stakeholders along the logistic and money flow pathway—purchasers (wholesalers, GPOs), intermediary decision-makers (HCPs, health systems, insurance providers), payers (employers, government, patients), and ultimately consumers (patients). It is increasingly recognized that these individual touch points need to be replaced by linked customer/patient journeys and it is necessary to understand and manage the relationships between formerly discrete customer channels. Introducing innovation into such a complex and rapidly evolving ecosystem requires the need to consider, understand, and potentially influence the entire ecosystem to find commercial success. Within this context, the industry can leverage new ventures that are regarded as adjacent innovation to shape the customer experience. Ones that are considered breakthrough innovation can be leveraged to create unique customer experiences.

Reflection: Shaping Customer Experience through Adjacent Innovation

To shape the customer experience through adjacent innovation, it is critical to understand the overall ecosystem within which customers will experience that innovation. This understanding is necessary to conceptualize the broadest impact of an adjacent innovation which may complement, challenge, or even modify the existing product or market. A digital therapeutic that can seamlessly plug into the daily processes and workflows of the broader healthcare ecosystem—whether the Electronic Health Record (EHR) at the hospital or smartphones, sensors and voice recognition systems in a smart home—will find rapid adoption and a high return due to universal adaptability. The more biopharmaceutical companies can do to help manage diseases through simple monitoring, alerts, and interventions, the less there would be the need for interactions with the healthcare delivery system of today.

This remote-monitoring and care management capability would enable the biopharmaceutical industry to expand its reach and impact across multiple sites of care thereby capturing a higher proportion of value within the healthcare ecosystem.

I (Ruchin), recently had the opportunity to meet with Kurt Graves at Intarcia Therapeutics. The company is working on ITCA 650—a small matchstick-sized combination drug/device-delivery system that can be implanted just under your skin for a period of six months and up to one year. Through the principles of osmosis, this device releases measured micro-doses of a drug over the time the device is implanted under the skin. The drug/device system is being tested for managing diabetes, obesity, and even the prevention of HIV. Through this innovation, the company is aiming to solve for one of the critical factors driving high healthcare costs in major chronic diseases—lack of medication adherence over time. By simplifying the process of adhering to medication, such a technology should also minimize ongoing interaction a patient requires with the healthcare ecosystem, and can hypothetically allow Intarcia Therapeutics to improve outcomes and capture a more significant share of value from the healthcare system. The company is also unique in that it has hired a Chief Design Officer and a Chief Experience Officer. These leaders are driving continuous improvement in the process of embedding the delivery device in the body by making the procedure faster, more comfortable, and as error-free as possible; this would obviously enhance both the provider and the patient experience. The process is designed to be modular in the sense that it can be executed similarly in a primary care physician's office or a retail clinic or a hospital, by a trained nurse practitioner. In our view, ITCA 650 is not only an example of a simple and modular product offering, but also of applying user-centered design principles to provide an excellent customer experience within the current healthcare ecosystem.

Reflection: Breakthrough Innovation to Capture Market Opportunity Created by a Hybrid Ecosystem

In the case of breakthrough innovation, it is essential either to understand the current ecosystem but then consciously "ignore" it in order to imagine a new (or better) ecosystem without placing constraints on the disruptive characteristics of the innovation.

We proposed the idea of S[i]M as an underlying value proposition that the biopharmaceutical industry can offer to remain a relevant player in the rapidly evolving hybrid human existence. We have discussed how almost every industry is undergoing a similar evolution. When I (Ruchin) came to the United States in 1995 to study, it cost two dollars per minute to call my parents back in India. Today, we regularly Facetime or Skype with our family in India for "free"—and they can participate in our son's cello recitals or graduation ceremonies remotely. We are waiting for the day when we can transmit delicacies we grew up on remotely as well! On the one hand, Virtual Reality (VR) scream rides are now offering a much safer way to experience the joys of a real roller-coaster without the risks of a mechanical failure and plunge to death. On the other, VR-based space-flight simulations are being used to prepare astronauts for journeys to Mars and deep-space exploration. One can get a prescription for contacts or eyeglasses without ever driving to an optometrist by accessing online services such as Opternative. Once armed with a prescription, we can even order custom eyeglasses from Warbey Parker or Zenni Optical. Fitnect provides for a fully virtual trial room where individuals can "try" garments without ever physically going to the store and physically picking up the garment from the racks. Groceries are now delivered to my doorstep, and Blue Apron defines how progressive we are in our culinary sophistication. The list goes on.

Earlier in Chapter 5, we introduced the concept of a potential new business model for the biopharmaceutical industry oriented toward the emergence of a Hybrid Human

Existence and provided examples of organizations that are experimenting with building capabilities that could fit with such an undertaking. The level 5 S[i]M as described in Table 4.2 envisions the goal of "healthy time" or "zero downtime" for patients as the ultimate goal in support of such a business model. We can all identify myriad intellectual, investment, logistics, and infrastructure challenges for incumbents to evolve toward such a business model. However, imagine a NewCo established on the principles of leveraging and building on everything positive about the incumbent industry model while simultaneously disrupting every aspect that is being challenged at an accelerating rate. Imagine a Central Nervous System (CNS) product offering consisting of an off-patent pharmaceutical product (or no conventional pharmaceutical at all) coupled with an individualized wellness and treatment regimen supported by a VR-enabled program of Cognitive Behavioral Therapy (CBT), meditation, healthy eating, and exercise. The NewCo markets this offering through partnerships with payers, organized providers, self-insured employers, and patients bypassing the traditional sales models focused on individual prescribers. The NewCo spawns the new S[i]M industry subsector!

While no one has perfected the art of engaging us in our increasingly real hybrid existence, the 80-80 Rule provides a useful framework for organizations interested in entering such new ventures. Incumbents, as well as new entrants, should realize that moving into adjacent and breakthrough spaces will require new learning and experimentation. It will require challenging the current understanding of consumption patterns and associated business model assumptions. They need to ensure there are systems in place to support it happening organically or, at a minimum, eliminating barriers that could get in the way. As we have discussed, one of the most significant challenges to non-product innovation in the biopharmaceutical industry is the current pricing and reimbursement system which, given its fragmentation and lack of transparency, has led to the Unicorn status many companies in the industry have achieved. While past success explains the current desire of the industry to maintain status quo in the payment models, we believe that innovation in pricing and reimbursement will become a critical success factor for driving core, adjacent, and breakthrough innovation in the future. The NewCo example referenced above provides an opportunity for such experimentation. One could envision a revenue model derived from the integrated offering that is tied only to producing the desired outcome versus being dependent on the sale of the product itself. Pricing of the offering could be based on cost offsets for other components of the healthcare value chain demonstrated by a transparent, flexible, and open model with variable inputs. Such a model could be customized to reflect underlying patient population dynamics and other elements that typically impact quality and cost of care in a particular geography and/or care setting but are usually ignored in a fragmented payment model. Rather than charging for components at the time utilization begins (the sale in the current model), one could envision no upfront costs. Instead, it has a subscription model whereby payment is tied to the achievement of pre-defined health improvement goals at the lowest possible cost. Most likely, this would involve a baseline charge adjusted up or down periodically. With sufficient data capture and machine learning capabilities regarding outcomes at both the individual patient and population levels, the cost of the integrated offering changes over time (positive or negative). If all parties could feel better about what they are spending or earning because the value and outcomes are transparent, we would be significantly ahead of the current situation where people argue about costs with little to no real understanding of value. While many execution challenges will need to be solved for and teaming the right talent will be critical to implementing any such pricing and reimbursement models successfully, we are optimistic that such future scenarios that shift the industry's business model are possible.

Chapter 10

Becoming Adept at Partnering

"Our success has really been based on partnerships from the very beginning."

Bill Gates

In the new age of healthcare characterized by rapid market changes, an evolving regulatory climate, advancement in technology, and the emergence of multiple new players, the biopharmaceutical industry will need to figure out how to become a partner across the healthcare ecosystem. It will need to move beyond its traditional boundaries and leverage collaborations and partnerships as new sources of value creation and competitive advantage.

Due to the competitive nature and the regulations related to pre-market promotion, the industry research and development processes tend to be tightly guarded and tend to solve for unmet therapeutic needs based on a population-level epidemiological view rather than true understanding of healthcare ecosystem needs. Furthermore, its sales management processes are focused on delivering (detailing) a narrowly defined message regarding the approved label of the product and negotiating contracts within pre-determined pricing and rebate bands. True customer centricity that can be achieved through co-creation of healthcare products and solutions with patients and customers is constrained due to regulation imposed upon the industry governing its interactions with the broader healthcare ecosystem. There is also a reluctance by most incumbents to challenge the status quo and explore alternative approaches given the historically successful Unicorn Industry model. The result is that the industry operates as a supplier and not a partner in the healthcare ecosystem. While this might have worked in the days when the industry's focus was on solving for diseases at the population level, the model is challenged in this age of personalization.

From an internal procurement perspective, the industry' relationships with its suppliers—from Clinical Research Organizations to marketing agencies to management consultants—tend to be transactional. The only time one sees examples of strategic partnerships in the industry is in the context of alliances and co-promotion agreements between two manufacturers. Seldom does one see strategic partnerships with stakeholders from outside the industry that require going beyond the comfort of traditional biopharmaceutical development and commercialization processes.

Over time, this has led to the development of a working model driven by standard operating procedures and talent competencies geared toward internally focused and one-sided engagements. As a result, the industry finds it difficult to work in partnerships with stakeholders outside the industry.

Given the rapid pace of change in the market and daily emergence of new technologies that can be applied in the business of the biopharmaceutical industry, the current core competencies of the industry fall short of the new competencies and approaches required for sustained competitive advantage. Proving safety and efficacy and securing regulatory approval used to be the end goals for biopharmaceutical products; today, they are the price of entry. Traditional methods to build new competencies based on training or talent acquisition take time. Partnerships, however, provide a quick path to such skills—where partners can come together or break away on a dynamic basis based on goals and needs.

As forces outside the industry continue to redefine and narrow the definition of value and commoditize traditional biopharmaceutical products, companies that can harness the power of partnerships in an agile fashion will create competitive advantage. Working collaboratively requires an open mind that each partner has something to offer that can be of mutual value. This assumption applies equally to initiatives focused on sustaining core business from the development and commercialization perspective, and to those focused on discovering new engines of growth. Assuming the biopharmaceutical industry recognizes and embraces this new approach to partnering across the healthcare ecosystem, success will require a similar openness to collaboration with other stakeholders. While pharma faces some challenges given the current climate surrounding pricing, our own experience in establishing payer and provider partnerships has confirmed a willingness across healthcare ecosystem players to explore potential opportunities to work together in new ways to solve for healthcare needs.

Dr. David Feinberg, CEO of the Geisinger Health System, is not impressed by the extent of healthcare improvement delivered by the major sector players—providers, payers, and pharma manufacturers. He points to disappointing examples observed in the U.S. healthcare system including the growing rate of obesity, failure to address mental health challenges, and substance abuse. He believes that no one group in the ecosystem can be successful on its own. In his view, all stakeholders need to be oriented toward the same "true North" around patient centeredness. He believes that the biopharmaceutical industry needs to be much more flexible in its approach to pricing—potentially even going to some risk sharing in the total cost of care. Ultimately, Dr. Feinberg believes biopharma must be "in the tent" to fully achieve healthcare improvement objectives, in contrast to a growing number of provider organizations who seek to exclude the industry from engagement.

Michael Dowling, CEO of Northwell Health, believes that the current healthcare landscape is too fragmented and that one way to achieve meaningful progress in improving healthcare is via provider-biopharmaceutical partnerships that transcend historical, transactional relationships. Mr. Dowling created a Pharma Ventures group within Northwell Health to facilitate such opportunities and demonstrate that "pharma is not the enemy." The team initially faced skepticism from Northwell Health physicians reflecting doubts about collaborating with biopharmaceutical companies. However, by having the Pharma Ventures group report into the Chief Operating Officer, a clear message was sent to the organization that the initiative was of high strategic importance, ensuring required priority and resource allocation while also establishing credibility with potential partners. Over the last few years, Mr. Dowling and the Northwell Health team have seen a gradual increase in the willingness of biopharma leaders to engage in discussions geared toward exploring new types of relationships including broader health improvement opportunities and reimbursement models where providers and biopharmaceutical companies receive a single outcome-based bundled payment versus getting reimbursed for the service and product separately. He also sees the opportunity for more collaborative research projects to address issues such as ensuring adequate representation of diverse populations in product development clinical trials.

Mr. Dowling also spoke about the need to improve relationships between provider systems and payers/health plans. Some of his perspectives have been shaped by Northwell Health's experience in setting up its health plan to compete in the Affordable Care Act (ACA) exchange, and employer-sponsored insurance sectors to participate more broadly in the healthcare value chain. The health plan also provided a vehicle for experimenting with new care delivery and payment models. While the venture faced challenges associated with some of the ACA regulations around risk adjustment, the experience has suggested additional opportunities for joint biopharma and health system engagement with payers.

Our conversations with both Dr. Feinberg and Mr. Dowling confirm that the Organized Customer Collaborations group that we established at Boehringer Ingelheim with a view toward transforming biopharmaceutical product development and commercialization through partnerships was a step in the right direction. As the healthcare ecosystem continues to evolve, companies that have figured out how to work in partnerships will have a competitive advantage. Cross-ecosystem partnerships can not only lead to the discovery of new business models but also ultimately drive human health.

Partnerships That Span Development and Commercialization

The healthcare consumer of the twenty-first century does not accept the traditional one-sided relationship with providers, payers, or suppliers in which they are just recipients of the decisions that have been made by others on their behalf. They are becoming more active participants in all aspects of their care versus merely being an end user. Providers are struggling to engage with patients. They are also struggling to understand and survive in an environment where the payment model is shifting from a fee-for-service structure to payment for quality and outcomes, where patient satisfaction scores become an essential driver of their compensation. Similarly, payers are finding it necessary to get more engaged in the delivery of care to be able to understand and influence new reimbursement models that can improve quality and drive down costs.

Biopharmaceutical manufacturers have recognized that even within their traditional growth engine—internal R&D—it is just not possible to rely purely on internal capabilities to compete in such an environment. As discussed before, they have increasingly turned to the outside via academic research, start-ups or crowdsourcing, and more open study designs to accelerate innovation. What has lagged behind is the recognition that a similar approach using new types of partnerships across multiple stakeholders in the value chain such as those we explored during our time at Boehringer Ingelheim can enable biopharma incumbents to transform their traditional development and commercialization models and find new ways to co-create IP, commercialize products, or create entirely new business opportunities and sources of revenue.

Working with patients early to understand their experiences and journey during diagnosis or treatment can suggest attributes that should be part of the traditional product itself and other innovative solutions that go beyond the molecule. Armed with in-house R&D insights regarding disease and treatment patterns and engaging with willing payers through formal arrangements versus one-off advisory boards early and throughout the development process can help ensure that products selected for development will meet future needs and deliver value as assessed by the customer. Similarly, conducting clinical development programs with provider networks that treat patients in real-world settings can accelerate the adoption of new technology following regulatory approval and help demonstrate how biopharmaceuticals can deliver cost offsets and outcomes relevant to provider reimbursement. Partnerships with new entrants from the technology industry can help accelerate the development process and develop new healthcare solutions ranging from adherence solutions all the way to S[i]M.

Moving one step further, in a future where S[i]M becomes the norm, enrolling patients and consumers who are comfortable accepting solutions that are viewed as a work in progress from the traditional perspective may be required to prototype and develop these products rapidly. This approach will require breaking away from the current static boundaries that exist between various healthcare stakeholders and regulators and becoming comfortable with active collaboration in pursuit of the best healthcare solutions. This approach will challenge biopharma's traditional thinking around a static versus rapidly iterating product label, associated downside risks, and product liability. Patient associations and advocacy groups are typically strongly motivated to make progress in finding cures, and as such, they can be engaged to overcome these potential barriers. This approach would also disrupt the traditional silos of biopharmaceutical product development followed by commercialization. In fact, product development can happen at a personal level with full customization. For example, the underlying biopharmaceutical product may be the same, but the digital interface and dosing regimen may be customized to the patient working in collaboration with the providers. Successful adoption would require that the regulatory framework continues to evolve (which we believe is already occurring), physicians are trained in new techniques and technology for treatment (which is also rapidly happening), and patients are willing to adopt them (we have not seen any evidence to the contrary).

In the near term, competitive advantage lies in the product, the services around the product that can potentially capture value by diminishing the need for traditional provider-centric care, and the relationships that allow scale-up of such products and services in the market (Figure 10.1). In an environment where time and cost of production continue to drop due to technology, and IP protections are limited in a global market, relationships that allow for rapid scale-up might provide a longer-lasting competitive advantage. For example, when Boehringer Ingelheim decided to evaluate the smart inhaler in the market to understand if providers would prescribe it, patients would use it,

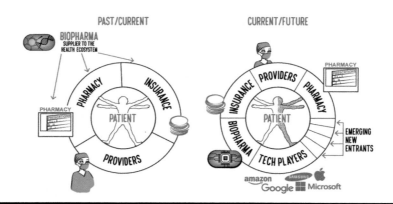

Figure 10.1   Future biopharmaceutical industry: from a healthcare ecosystem supplier to a fully engaged partner.

and whether it could deliver better outcomes, a warm reception was received for testing the concept at the C-level leadership and with leading physicians at major hospitals. Despite the initial positive reactions to the idea, what became apparent soon after was that to make the solution work in the real world, it needed to be integrated into the clinical workflow and IT infrastructure of these health systems. Driving such integration required a different competency than biopharma typically has. Embedding these solutions into clinical workflows and working in partnership with customers would enable co-creation of a repetitive process blueprint that could be leveraged to integrate future smart solutions. Over time, such alliances would create the competencies, relationships, and trust that are required to carve out a competitive edge in the market. These kinds of partnerships embody what Professor Edmondson characterizes as "extreme teaming."

Making Partnerships Work

What we discussed above are just a few simple examples. However, the process to incorporate these partnerships into business as usual for incumbent industry participants is not easy. All partnerships take time to carefully define mutual goals, see a collective vision of the future, and build trust and a truly collaborative work environment. Defining ownership of intellectual property and clarity on specific contributions from each side become topics of lengthy deliberation. Given the biopharmaceutical industry's historical approach of complete ownership of intellectual property and considering partners as vendors, legal contracting processes tend to drag on. The regulatory framework within which the industry operates requires proper due diligence to ensure full compliance and that partnerships don't become a conduit for illicit commercial activity. Often, finding common ground requires more internal negotiation within companies than bargaining with outside companies. Breaking down such barriers within incumbents is difficult but is the key to future success.

When approaching partnerships and collaborations, the 80-80 Rule principles should be applied as a means to fill competency gaps and build new sources of value and competitive advantage. The partnerships should first be viewed with a clear vision of mutual benefit and trust. What is also a given is that when you enter a partnership, it will be impossible to envision every future scenario (positive or negative). Trying to anticipate every plausible possibility and assigning an equal level of risk to events that are more certain to happen than others only prolongs the legal contracting process.

Similarly, as teams start to form and operate across stakeholders, the 80-80 Rule should be kept front and center. Within the boundaries of a corporation, where purpose and culture tend to be cohesive, forming effective teams can be a challenge. When stakeholders across different companies have to work in teams rather than in a more traditional buyer–supplier relationship, very different purpose and cultures of respective organizations add to the complexity of effective teaming. Overcoming this complexity requires embracing the 80-80 Rule mindset, where experimentation, openness to uncertainty, willingness to learn from the new, and discovering the unanticipated must be prioritized over standard operating procedures and traditional ways of doing things. Developing such a mindset requires not only individual acumen, but also deliberate talent development processes where experimentation and teaming skills are prioritized over deep specialization.

Ultimately, it is about the mindset. We advocate that the industry embraces the fact that it has to prepare for a future where the competitive advantages of the "Unicorn Industry" no longer exist. It has to redefine innovation to find new engines of growth deliberately. And it has to fire on all cylinders for new growth platforms to emerge and persist. The 80-80 Rule—being 80% confident that you will only be 80% right the first time should feel normal—is the new mindset that needs to percolate throughout the industry. It can then break away from the traditional business model, overcome the impending disruption, and retain its place as a value driver in the healthcare ecosystem.

Chapter 11

Afterword

Philip Morris International announced a dramatic New Year resolution for 2018: "We're trying to give up cigarettes." This announcement represents a dramatic strategic shift for the company, a departure from the historical business of cigarettes to explore new revenue opportunities within the tobacco industry. Only time will tell if the biopharmaceutical industry makes a similar resolution to move away from traditional biopharmaceutical products and the associated business model.

In the meantime, it seems that between early 2017 when we embarked on the effort to write this book, and now, the crisis within the biopharmaceutical industry that we highlight in our work has accelerated. There is not even a single day that goes by without news of another incumbent in the industry experiencing a setback in their product pipeline or commercial expectations. Reports of restructuring and mass layoffs have become so routine that they no longer register as unique anymore. The dialogue on perceived excessive pricing of pharmaceutical products seems to have increased in tempo. The FDA, under a new Commissioner, has signaled willingness to examine pharmaceutical pricing in the context of a public health issue. The new Health and Human Services

(HSS) Secretary (a former industry insider) has vowed to look at stemming the rate of increase in drug prices and has proposed that Medicare Part B should be allowed to negotiate drug prices directly. The most recent Presidential budget proposal shifts the Affordable Care Act requirement to cover a portion of patients' pharmaceutical costs once they hit the Medicare Part D coverage gap or "donut hole" from health plans to manufacturers, thus increasing pharma's total contribution to 70% of the patients' coverage gap further negatively impacting margins. Ballot initiatives at the state level to stem drug prices are increasingly being introduced and passed. The increased rate of consolidation between provider systems and vertical integration between PBMs, payers, and providers is creating purchasing behemoths that can negotiate better prices. The climate for the biopharmaceutical industry continues to deteriorate.

While there is a flow of positive news regarding the continued promise of digital technologies and digital medicine, we have not yet seen any clear shift by incumbents toward a sustained innovation effort to explore business model alternatives that go beyond the molecule as the underlying source of value. Most investments and even novel, cross-industry partnerships remain oriented toward preserving the status quo. For example, a recent announcement by AstraZeneca regarding its partnership with Ali Health, a subsidiary of Alibaba in China, focuses on enabling patients to find and stay on the right medicines. The deal with Tencent focuses on ensuring integrity of supply chain to fight counterfeit medicines. As we have discussed, the "Unicorn Industry" status that the biopharmaceutical sector has attained continues to be the most significant internal barrier for incumbents toward doing anything differently.

New entrants to the biopharmaceutical industry, seem to fall into two broad categories. There are the those that are looking to simulate the existing unicorn business model to drive economic returns from the next "molecule." Then there are others that are developing new therapies such as digital therapeutics and other alternative therapies. However, rather than pushing for business model innovation, they are looking to mirror the clinical trials and other established protocols of the traditional biopharmaceutical industry. The goal is to capture significant reimbursement potential leveraging Current Procedural Terminology (CPT), International Classification of Diseases (ICD), or the Healthcare Common Procedure Coding System (HCPCS) based J codes. It is still rare to find examples of companies that are reimagining not only the offering, but also the reimbursement models.

On the other hand, generational shifts are finally beginning to impact consumption patterns in the markets. While the baby boomer generation is still the largest consumer, it is starting to decline in numbers and influence in fueling demand for new products and services. The millennials are coming of age and are becoming the primary market segment. We discussed earlier that millennials are considered digital natives; that is, they have grown up with digital technology from an early age and are therefore not only comfortable with it, but also expect it to shape their daily life. As for the emerging Gen Z—the digital innates where digital is part of their inherent cognitive conscience—the hybrid existence between the biological and the digital realms and associated expectations for products and services is more real than ever.

In general, millennials have lesser buying power than baby boomers. There is also emerging evidence that Gen Z's future will be one where "jobs" with fixed employers as we know them today will have disappeared and been largely replaced by independent contractors bidding on work, individually or as part of virtual teams. Buying power will be even lower than that of millennials, and technology will continue to drive globalization of labor pools and markets. We recently had a firsthand experience to support this thesis. As we were looking for an illustrator to help us bring to life some of the proposed concepts in this book, we initially contacted local artists; however, they were not able to commit to the timeline we had. We looked at alternative options, and ultimately found Hanna Tamsalu-Orlova, who is based in Estonia, through a global marketplace for freelancers called Upwork. Not only was she willing to complete the project within our required timeframe, but we also realized that Upwork allowed us to choose between artists whose hourly rates ranged from $10/hour to $50/hour. We found that the hourly rates were driven primarily by geographic location of the artist, and not the level of their training or quality of their work. With technology enabling such a global marketplace, it is only a matter of time before the wage differences across the globe will start to disappear, and standard of living equalize. In such a scenario, we may see an emergence of a "globally equal" poor, middle, and upper class. In such a future, country-based reimbursement rates for healthcare may become a relic of the past, replaced by equalization across the globe. Employer-sponsored health insurance will most likely become a historical fact. Globally, we may see a universal trend where the bulk of the population will become dependent on a publicly-financed system of healthcare. China and India, two economies that are forecasted to overtake the United States in the next 20 years, are already predominantly public-health-financing focused. Japan and the rest of the developed countries will continue to drive this trend further. Of course, there will always be the usual global pool of the "top 1%" who can afford whatever healthcare they want.

We firmly believe that in the future world inhabited by digital natives and digital innates, technology will continue to drive price transparency and potential global normalization of healthcare financing. Such transparency will disrupt the Unicorn Industry business model of today, and the biopharmaceutical industry will have to play a different game. S[i]M that treats digital inhabitants in their simultaneous biological and virtual world is one option that could allow biopharmaceutical companies not only to remain a relevant stakeholder, but also to capture at least some elements of the healthcare value chain held today by other stakeholders such as providers and insurers. Companies that can successfully crack the code on "Zero Downtime for Patients" and move away from a "product fill"-based reimbursement model to annuity-based models might find higher commercial success. We look forward to the future where the question "Have you taken your medicine?" is replaced by the question "Have you taken your S[i]M?" That would indicate to us that the biopharmaceutical industry has evolved and integrated itself firmly in impacting patient health, and the new industry sub-sector we have proposed is firmly in place.

Some may say that our recommendations for the future evolution of the biopharmaceutical industry are more of the same or not disruptive enough. In our view, some organizations may adopt an approach that may qualify as "pragmatic transformation," while others may discover new ways to disrupt. Our goal is to spur that thinking and encourage enough people to challenge the status quo. We anticipate that our work will create a disruptive dialogue within the biopharmaceutical industry and be the trigger for the level of change we would like to see and believe to be necessary to preserve the contributions of such a historically vital and impactful industry. We foresee a future where medical science is so highly evolved that diseases are cured with a single intervention. In that scenario, the concept of S[i]M and Zero Downtime for Patients may become a relic of the past. New business models will emerge. In the interim, we hope that the analytical frameworks we have discussed here regarding innovation beyond the core, and the principles related to Setting Up for Success, Finding White Spaces, Developing New Ventures, and Becoming Adept at Partnering, will sustain themselves over time.

Others may ponder as to why and how the 80-80 Rule is relevant in this context. As we have noted before, the transformation of businesses, industries or nations requires a fundamental shift in mindset. It is certain that the future will be different from today, but the path to it is uncertain. Therefore, there will always be those who would prefer to preserve the known comfort of the status quo. But then there are also those who will strive for more. In our minds, human evolution is attributed to those who push boundaries. We hope that the 80-80 Rule gets adopted as a defining philosophy and the mindset for those who are pragmatic yet courageous, willing to experiment knowing the risks, explore and strive for more.

Beyond having the right philosophical approach and mindset, we are fully aware that it is competent execution that leads to good future outcomes. Competent execution requires visionary yet pragmatic leadership that dares to disrupt the status quo and steer the course toward new futures. The 80-80 Rule is an embodiment of that mindset.

While the origins for and examples illustrating the 80-80 Rule are informed by our direct experiences in the biopharmaceutical industry, the philosophy and principles apply to other healthcare sectors as well. The overall healthcare landscape that we have outlined in our work is creating similar pressures for every incumbent player in the industry. These include medical devices and diagnostics manufacturers, payers, providers, pharmacy benefit managers, retail pharmacy chains. With their traditional business models and profitability under siege and growth opportunities becoming increasingly scarce, they are looking at mergers and acquisitions as well as vertical integration (payers–providers, pharmacy chains–insurers–alternate sites of care, etc.) for future sustainability. Similar to the biopharmaceutical industry, they are exploring how digital technologies can be harnessed to drive better customer engagement and transform their current core processes— from clinical workflows to advanced, predictive data analytics to matching the right products and services to the right customers. Others are looking at global expansion, either through affiliations or outright acquisitions. An effort by a group of hospital systems to set up their own not-for-profit generics manufacturing facility is another example of blurring the traditional boundaries between healthcare stakeholders. Many other incumbents will be forced to examine their competitive positioning in the market as endeavors such as the recently announced collaboration between Amazon, J.P. Morgan Chase, and Berkshire Hathaway to provide technology enabled healthcare to their employees lead to the development of new, unanticipated healthcare business models. As these healthcare organizations explore their futures, they can adopt the innovation opportunity framework we have proposed to deliberately define an innovation agenda to drive their future sustainability and growth.

In almost every other incumbent industry we look at, from financial services to manufacturing to consumer staples, digital shifts are fundamentally disrupting the old business models. Autonomous cars are on the roads, and the automobile industry is experimenting with a transportation-as-a-service model to replace product-based selling model. "BOOK" by Cadillac offers its customers an option to drive any of the Cadillac cars on demand for a monthly fixed fee. Blockchain-based cryptocurrencies have befuddled the stock markets and caught the attention of regulators. In fact, even 130-year-old Kodak may have learned from its earlier disruption by digital imagery and has launched its own cryptocurrency, Kodakcoin, to facilitate buying and selling of photographs and monitor improper use. These initiatives challenge the status quo business models of incumbent industries and must have required leadership courage and foresight to craft new futures.

While no one has the crystal ball, paradoxically, two future events are certain—death and the disruption of the status quo. While immortality remains the holy grail, we are convinced that getting ahead of disruption is well within the capacity of the human race. We are also convinced that despite the forces that caution us against an overdependence on technology so we can remain "human," the human race will continue to accelerate its technological evolution.

The recipe for success in such a future will differ by industry. We are however convinced that it will uniformly require broadening the definition, sources, and enablers of innovation beyond what led to their respective historical success. Business models will need to evolve faster than the market. A new breed of leadership that embraces the 80-80 Rule will be required to build new capabilities and drive culture change necessary to ignite growth.

Authors

Ruchin Kansal   In 2016, Medical Marketing & Media recognized Ruchin with a Top 40 Healthcare Transformers Award in 2016. According to the judges, "You can probably count on one hand the number of top-level pharma execs with an academic background in architecture. Yet, listening to Kansal talk about his role at BI—and in particular, about his progressive approach to effecting change within the digital and customer-relationship realms—you start to wonder if the creative, open-minded architect mindset may be a perfect fit for circa-2016 healthcare."

Ruchin is the Managing Director of Kansal & Co, a think tank focused on innovation, consulting and new ventures in the healthcare industry. As a health industry executive and advisor, he has experience in developing growth strategies, launching new ventures, building digital health businesses, incubating strategic partnerships, and igniting innovation and transformation within large corporations. He established and led the first Business Innovation division at Boehringer Ingelheim Pharmaceuticals Inc. In this role, he was responsible for setting and managing a company-wide growth-focused innovation agenda, establishing the company's first Digital Health team and commercially launching the first smart inhaler, building ecosystem collaborations with customers to co-create health solutions and competitive advantage, and driving culture change. Prior, as a C-level management consultant, he served Fortune 500 healthcare organizations in the United States, Japan, the European Union, and India. This experience provided him with a strong understanding of the healthcare ecosystem and its business transactions.

In his early years, he trained as an architect and developed a strong foundation in the principles of design thinking and user-centered design. In his graduate work completed in 1997 when the Internet was still in its infancy, he proposed the concept of a cybernetic agora—a hybrid physical/virtual space for public discourse—as a basis for digital ventures of today.

Ruchin has served on the Board of Stanford Medicine X and was invited to the White House OSTP to share ideas on engaging participants as partners in research. He received his MBA from NYU-Stern, master's degree from Kansas State University, and bachelor's degree from IIT, Roorkee, India. He has completed leadership training at Duke University and Kunshan University, China.

Ruchin can be contacted at ruchin.kansal@the8080rule.com for any questions or to discuss speaking engagements.

Jeff Huth   With more than 35 years in the biopharmaceutical industry in a broad range of roles from pre-clinical research to marketing and sales management in the United States and the European Union, Jeff has seen it all. He has personally witnessed the pharmaceutical industry go from one held in high regard by the public and customers and the darling of Wall Street to one that is increasingly portrayed as a villain and misses financial targets.

At Boehringer Ingelheim, Jeff held leadership roles including Sr. VP and Head of the Primary Care Business Unit,

Sr. VP of Market Access, and Sr. VP of Marketing. He was asked by the U.S. CEO and Corporate Board to lead the most extensive transformation initiative undertaken across the entire U.S. company including the adoption of a new commercial model. This experience re-enforced the massive change in environment and market dynamics being faced by today's biopharmaceutical industry and highlighted the need for a new way of defining what it takes to succeed.

Jeff was Boehringer Ingelheim's longtime representative to the National Pharmaceutical Council (NPC) and Board Chairman in 2014. In this capacity, he was able to help shape the industry's thinking about evidence-based medicine and the need to demonstrate value more broadly.

Since his retirement from Boehringer Ingelheim, Jeff now spends his time advising clients in the biopharmaceutical industry with a focus on market access and commercial model transformation.

Jeff has undergraduate and graduate degrees in Biological Sciences supplemented by Executive Development programs at Ashridge, INSEAD, and the University of Michigan.

Jeff can be contacted at jeff.huth@the8080rule.com for any questions or to discuss speaking engagements.

Index

PGSTL 05/16/2018